THE CATHOLIC UNIVERSITY OF AMERICA

CANON LAW STUDIES

NO. 315

SACRED FURNISHINGS OF CHURCHES

BY

REV. ERWIN L. SADLOWSKI, M.A., J.C.L.

Priest of the Diocese of Spokane

A Dissertation

SUBMITTED TO THE FACULTY OF THE SCHOOL OF CANON LAW OF THE CATHOLIC UNIVERSITY OF AMERICA IN PARTIAL FULFILLMENT OF THE REQUIREMENTS FOR THE DEGREE OF DOCTOR OF CANON LAW

THE CATHOLIC UNIVERSITY OF AMERICA

WASHINGTON, D. C.

1951

NIHIL OBSTAT:
Eduardus Roelker, S.T.D., J.C.D.,
Censor Deputatus

IMPRIMATUR:
Carolus D. White, D.D.,
Episcopus Spokanensis

Spokane, die 2 junii, 1950

TO THE MEMORY
OF MY MOTHER AND FATHER

TABLE OF CONTENTS

TABLE OF CONTENTS—Continued

TABLE OF CONTENTS—Continued

ILLUSTRATIONS

FOREWORD

It is the purpose of this dissertation to examine the legislation on the sacred furnishings of Churches as it was contained in the *Corpus Iuris Canonici* and as it is contained today in the Code of Canon Law, in the Liturgical Books, and in the Decrees of the Congregation of Rites. Historically, it could appear that there is a lacuna covering the period from the time of the Council of Trent to the time of the promulgation of the Code of Canon Law in 1918; however, it should be remembered that much of the law regarding the sacred furnishings is contained in the Liturgical Books, published originally in the latter part of the sixteenth century, and in the Decrees of the Sacred Congregation of Rites, dating back to 1588.

Regarding the title "The Sacred Furnishings of Churches," it is proper to point out that it is used as the translation of the title *"De Sacra Supellectili,"* comprising Canons 1296-1306 of the Code of Canon Law. This section of the Code, with few exceptions, does not go into detail regarding particular sacred furnishings, but treats of them in a general way, i.e., as applicable to all of the sacred furnishings. The commentary on this section of the Code will comprise Part Two, Section One, of this dissertation. Part Two, Section Two, will treat of the sacred furnishings in particular; its chief sources are the Liturgical Books and the Decrees of the Sacred Congregation of Rites.

It is from Canon 1296 that the notion of sacred furnishings was drawn, namely, as those things which are used for public worship, in particular those which are blessed or consecrated for this purpose. It should be noted that the Code in this section treats only of such furnishings as are distinct from the church itself and its permanent or immovable fixtures or furnishings such as the altar, tabernacle, confessionals, baptismal font, etc., which are treated in other sections of the Code; by the phrase "sacred furnishings" in this section are to be understood the portable or movable furnishings of the church.

In so far as it remains possible and practicable, the order of the Code of Canon Law will be followed.

The writer takes this occasion to express his gratitude to His Excellency, the Most Rev. Charles D. White, D.D., Bishop of Spokane, for the opportunity to pursue advanced studies in Canon Law; to the members of the Faculty of the School of Canon Law, The Catholic University of America, for their guidance and assistance in the preparation of this work; to his fellow students and all the others who made his course of study at the University valuable as well as pleasant.

PART ONE

THE LAW REGARDING THE SACRED FURNISHINGS IN THE *CORPUS IURIS CANONICI*

Introduction

At the time of the compilation of the *Decretum Gratiani* there was no definition of the sacred furnishings of churches as they are indicated today in the *Codex Iuris Canonici;*[1] however, it can be safely stated that those things which are considered as sacred furnishings at the present time were already well known and extant in the twelfth century. Thus, for example, such an ancient document as the *Constitutiones Apostolorum* had a prescription against the profane use of the sacred vessels and sacred vestments.[2]

The *Ordo Romanus,* too, knew the principal furnishings at least; it contained the following blessings and consecrations: for the linens; for the sacred vessels, linens, and instruments for use in the church or on the altar; for the priestly vestments; for the corporal; for the vessels used for the celebration of the Holy Eucharist; the consecration of the chalice and the paten.[3]

In the group of Ordinals collected by Hittorp (d. 1584), another work, which was composed in the latter part of the eighth century, devoted one chapter to the "Individual Vestments," and another to the "Significance of the Vestments."[4]

1 Liber Tertius, *De Rebus,* Pars Tertia, *de cultu divino,* Titulus XVIII *de sacra supellectili,* canon. 1296-1306. Note: throughout this work, the term "*sacra supellex*" will be translated as "sacred furnishings."

2 Canon 72.

3 Cf. *Ordo Romanus, Ordo de aedificanda ecclesia,* [in the compilation of Melchior Hittorpius, *De Catholicae Ecclesiae Divinis Officiis ac Ministeriis Varii Vetustorum fere Ominum Ecclesiae Patrum ac Scriptorum Libri,* (Rome, 1591) pp. 84-86.] Cf. also Michel Andrieu, *Les* Ordines Romani *du Haut Moyen Age,* (Louvain, "Spicilegium Sacrum Lovaniense, Bureaux, 1931), pp. 38, 170, 186.

4 Almarius F. Alcuinus, *Liber de Divinis Officiis,* pp. 63-65.

Two writers of the ninth century, whose works appeared in the same collection of Hittorp, gave further proof that even at that time most of the sacred furnishings were known. Rabanus Maurus (d. 856) devoted several chapters to the meaning of the various vestments.[5] Walafrid Strabo (d. 849) wrote a chapter on the consideration of "The Sacred Vessels and Sacred Furnishings."[6]

The *Rationale* of Durandus (1237-1296) made mention of practically all of the sacred furnishings which are known in the Church of the Latin Rite today.[7]

With regard to liturgical law in general, Bouix (1808-1870) pointed out the following observations regarding its binding force: during the first four centuries, the legislation on the liturgy was *de facto* almost entirely local, i.e., left to the jurisdiction of the local ordinary; in the fifth century it came under the jurisdiction of the metropolitan; from that time to the eighth century the Roman Pontiffs urged the observance of a universal liturgy.[8]

In fact a universal liturgy cannot be said to have existed before the time of St. Pius V (1566-1572).

> From the time of St. Gregory's revision of the local Roman rite, c. A.D. 595, to that of S. Pius V undertaken at the request of the Council of Trent nearly 1000 years later, no Pope ever officially touched the Roman ordinary. After Alcuin's revision just before A.D. 800 there was never a further official edition put out for general use before the Pian missal.[9]

---

[5] *De Institutione Clericorum,* Liber I, Capita 14-22.

[6] *De Exordiis et Incrementis Rerum Ecclesiasticarum,* Cap. 24.

[7] Gulielmus Durandus, *Rationale Divinorum Officiorum* (Neapoli, 1859), Liber I, Cap. II, no. 12 *Linteamina alba operiunt altare;* Cap. III, *De picturis, et cortinis, et ornamentis ecclesiae;* Liber Tertius: *De Indumentis seu ornamenta ecclesiae sacerdotum atque pontificum et aliorum ministrorum.*

[8] Dominique Bouix, *Tractatus de. Iure Liturgico* (3 ed., Parisiis, 1873), pars 3a, Cap. 1-4, pp. 157-171.

[9] Gregory Dix, *The Shape of the Liturgy* (Westminster: Dacre Press, 1946), p. 586.

CHAPTER I

THE LAW ON THE SACRED FURNISHINGS IN GRATIAN

The *Decree* of Gratian did not contain a concise treatment about the sacred furnishings of churches such as is found in the Code today. Rather, the matter concerning the sacred furnishings found its treatment in various places in Gratian's compilation, as being more or less incidental to other problems. Most of the material, however, is to be found in two sections: under canons 39-46, D. I, *de cons.*, and under several canons in D. XIII of Part One of the *Decree.*

An appropriate introduction to the law on the sacred furnishings in Gratian is the quotation of the following canon:

> . . . For if the Jews, who served in the shadow of the law, did these things, so much the more should we, to whom the truth has been revealed, to whom grace and truth have been given through Jesus, build churches for the Lord, and in as far as we can, decorate them better; we should devoutly and solemnly consecrate them together with their altars, vessels, vestments and other utensils used for divine services, with divine prayers and holy anointings; we should not celebrate Mass nor offer sacrifices to the Lord in any vessels not consecrated to the Lord by the Bishops . . .[1]

Although no definition of sacred furnishings can be found in the *Decree* of Gratian, it seems safe to assume the definition now indicated in the Code of Canon Law, viz., all those things which are used for public worship, especially such as are blessed or consecrated according to the laws of the liturgy.[2] Such a definition

[1] C. 2, D. I, *de cons.;* this canon is a *palea* found substantially in Burchard: III, 58; and Ivo, Decr. III, 61-Migne, *Patrologiae Cursus Completus,* Series Latina (221 vols., Parisiis, 1844-1864). (Hereafter this work will be cited as *MPL.*) For this reference cf. *MPL,* CXL, 683 and CLXI, 211. It is ascribed to a Pope Felix, cf. Paulus Hinschius, *Decretales Pseudo-Isidorianae* (Lipsiae, 1883), p. 698. (Hereafter this work will be cited as Hinschius.)

[2] Canon 1296, §1.

would correspond well to the statement above ". . . we should devoutly and solemnly consecrate . . . (the) vessels, vestments, and other utensils used for divine services . . ." In general, then, the term could be said to include any vessels, vestments, or other utensils which were blessed or consecrated for use in divine services.

The first legislation or law which will be considered is that which concerned the materials from which the sacred furnishings were to be made. On this point a division must be borne in mind, namely, between the sacred vessels (the chalice and the paten) and the sacred vestments, by which were meant precisely only the corporal, the pall, and the altar cloths, not including the vestments which the priest wore.

With regard to the sacred vessels, the use of wooden chalices was forbidden in a canon of a ninth century council.[3] This canon, upon a brief history of the matter, referred to the famous quip of St. Boniface: "At one time golden priests used wooden chalices, now wooden priests use gold chalices."[4] Pope St. Zepherinus (199-217) had ordered that glass patens be used; Pope Urban I (220-230) required all the sacred vessels to be of silver.[5] The Council of Tribur (from which the canon is taken) went on to order that from that time forth no priest should presume to celebrate the Holy Mystery of the Body and Blood of Christ in wooden vessels, "lest where God is to be pleased, instead He be angered."

The glossator noted that this prohibition did not touch the validity of the Mass, for the consecration did not depend on the vessel

[3] C. 44, D. I, *de cons.;* canon authentic from the Council of Tribur (895) c. 18; cf. Mansi, *Sacrorum Conciliorum Nova et Amplissima Collectio,* 53 vols. in 60, (Parisiis, 1901-1927) Vol. XVIII, p. 142. Hereafter this work will be referred to as Mansi.

[4] Cf. also Walafrid Strabo, *De Exordiis et Incrementis Rerum Ecclesiasticarum* (in edition of Hittorpius, *De Ecclesiae Divinis Officiis* etc., *supra* p. 1) cap. 24, where the history was summarized in a similar manner. This is of special interest in view of the fact that Strabo was born in 806 at Fulda, and educated there. Hence the works and sayings of St. Boniface could readily be familiar to him.

[5] Elsewhere no trace of such early papal legislation could be found.

but rather on the words of consecration, as was evident from the canon which dealt with the consecration of the Mass itself.[6]

Canon 45, D. I, *de cons.*, was more specific regarding the materials which were to be used for the manufacture of the chalice and paten. Three materials could be used licitly: gold was preferred; lacking this, silver was suitable; and finally, if the priest was too poor to be able to afford a chalice of gold or silver he was to have, at the very worst, one made of tin.[7]

Brass and copper chalices were forbidden for the very sensible reason that wine caused a rust or oxidization, which in turn was likely to produce nausea and vomit. Wooden or glass chalices were absolutely forbidden to be used for the celebration of Mass. The *glossa ordinaria* pointed out the very evident reasons for the proscription of the last two mentioned materials. Wood is porous, preventing the complete consumption of the Precious Blood; glass, on the other hand, is very fragile, exposing the Precious Blood to the very serious danger of being spilled.[8]

The sacred linens were to be made of pure linen or woven flax.[9] The gloss on the canon made it clear that the "*pannus*" mentioned therein was the corporal.[10] The altar cloths, too, were to be included.[11] Colored and silk materials were forbidden to be used as the altar linens for the celebration of Mass. The reason given for the exclusive use of linen for the sacred vestments was the fol-

[6] Cf. *glossa* s.v. *utuntur* on c. 44, D. I, *de cons.*, which gloss in turn referred back to c. 72, D. 2, *de cons.*

[7] Given as can. 6 of a Council of Rheims; cf. Mansi, X, 603, who indicates that this canon was added by Burchard, Ivo, and Gratian.

[8] Cf. *glossa* s.v. *in ligneo* and *vitreo* in c. 45, D. I, *de cons.*

[9] C. 46, D. I, *de cons.;* spurious canon taken from the *Excerpta ex Synodalibus Gestis Sancti Silvestri Papae;* cf. Hinschius, p. 450; also P. Jaffé, *Regesta Pontificum Romanorum ab condita Ecclesia ad annum post Christum natum MCXCVIII,* (2am ed. correctam et auctam auspiciis Gulielmi Wattenbach curaverunt F. Kaltenbrunner (ad annum 590), P. Ewald (590-882), S. Loewenfeld (882-1198), 2 vols., in 1, Lipsiae, 1885-1888). Hereafter this work will be referred to as Jaffé K (Kaltenbrunner), Jaffé E (Ewald), and Jaffé L (Lowenfeld). Cf. Jaffé K, no. 168.

[10] Cf. *glossa* s.v. *consulto* on c. 46, D. I, *de cons.*

[11] Cf. *glossa* s.v. *altaris palla* on c. 39, D. I, *de cons.*

lowing: the Body of Christ was buried in a winding sheet of pure linen. The gloss noted, too, that pure linen denotes innocence and purity; "*terreno*" was taken to signify that Christ assumed real mortal flesh from the Blessed Virgin Mary, His Mother, flesh capable of suffering. Finally, linen made of flax was prescribed, for just as flax by means of many flayings becomes white and lustrous, so Christ by many sufferings came into His glory, and so, too, will the good by many sufferings arrive at the glory of God.[12]

In another canon a special provision was laid down regarding the material from which the sacred linens were to be made. The words of the canon themselves seem to have meant that the sacred vestments *(mysteria)* were not to be used as wedding ornaments or wedding clothes.[13]

The gloss on this canon concluded from this also that chasubles or other church furnishings were not to be made from the garments of a married woman *(domina)*. The reason for the prohibition was explained as follows: such materials, having been defiled by the touch of the unjust or of worldly luxuries, would seem to be unbecoming for the exercise of the sacred mysteries.[14]

Whose particular duty it was to furnish the church, or to see to the preservation and safekeeping of the sacred furnishings, was not made clear in the *Decree* of Gratian. The only indication of whom such duties might be incumbent upon was the mention of the church treasurer *(thesaurarius)*. Even in this case the provision of the furnishings and the care of the furnishings was not mentioned.[15]

[12] Cf. *glossa* s.v. *sed in puro,* and *terreno,* and *lino* on c. 46, D. I, *de cons.;* cf. also Alcuinus, *Liber de Divinis Officiis,* Cap. *de Celebratione Missae et eius Significatione* (*edit. cit.* of Hittorpius), p. 70; who used the same line of reasoning relative to the purpose of the exclusive use of linen for the sacred vestments.

[13] C. 43, D. I, *de cons.;* canon authentic from the Council of Auvergne (535); cf. *Monumenta Germaniae Historica,* Legum Sectio III, Tomus I. *Concilia Aevi Merovingici* (recensuit Fredericus Maassen) (Hanoverae, 1893) p. 76.

[14] Cf. *glossa* s.v. *ad nuptiarum* on c. 43, D. I, *de cons.*

[15] C. 1, D. 25; this canon is taken from a letter of St. Isidore of Seville to Ludifred; cf. *MPL,* LXXXIII, 894.

It is disappointing that the gloss on this canon did not enlarge on the point, particularly in view of the fact that the canon is taken from a letter of St. Isidore of Seville (d. 636), who in another work pointed to the duties of the custodian *(officium custodis): "Custodes sacrarii Levitae sunt. Ipsis enim jussum est custodire tabernaculum et omnia vasa templi."*[16]

In the *Decree* of Gratian itself, the only indication relative to the safekeeping of the sacred furnishings was the statement in c. 40, D. I, *de cons.*, which pointed out that the "ministers" were commanded to safeguard diligently the sacred linens in the sacristy. No explanation was offered in the text itself nor in the glosses as to who these "ministers" were.

Worn out vestments and other sacred furnishings that were not longer usable for divine services were to be burnt.[17] This law included all of the sacred furnishings, corporals, altar cloths, *cortinae*, candlesticks.[18]

The reason which was given for this law is applicable even today, namely, to prevent the profanation of sacred things which have been used for divine services. Even the ashes were to be disposed of in such a way as to preclude all profanation. Three places were suggested for their disposal: the baptistry (meaning undoubtedly the drain therein), a wall, or the *"fossae pavimentorum."* It is difficult to determine the exact meaning of the last mentioned term; literally, it means "the trenches under the flagstones." This would indeed have precluded any trampling by foot, but it would not have precluded profanation. Possibly a logical explanation would rather

[16] *De Ecclesiasticis Officiis*, Cap. IX, Lib. 2, *De Custodibus Sacrorum—MPL*, LXXXIII, 790.

[17] C. 39, D. I, *de cons.;* spurious canon. It is taken from the Letter of Pope St. Clement to James, the brother of the Lord; cf. Jaffé K, No. 11, and Hinschius, p. 46. Although patrologists are generally agreed that this letter is not one of Clement's, nonetheless it is of very ancient origin, fourth century eastern copies of it having been found; cf. Steidle, *Patrologia* (Friburgi: Herder and Co., 1937), p. 13, n. 6. It is also found under the title *Praecepta S. Petri de Sacramentis conservandis*, in the works of St. Leo the Great—*MPL*, LVI, 675.

[18] Cf. *glossa* s.v. *altaris palla* and *velum* on c. 39, D. I, *de cons.*

point to a dry well lined with stones, similar to the modern *sacrarium.*

The *Decree* of Gratian expounded legislation not so much on the use of the sacred furnishings as on their misuse. One matter in particular received special attention—the burial of the dead in the vestments of the altar. No cleric was to permit the dead to be buried in such vestments.[19] It seems evident in this case that by "vestments" the canon meant to include only what are known as sacred vestments, i.e., the corporal and the altar cloths. The glosses on this canon and the preceding one made this quite clear.[20] If this is accepted, then the gloss on the meaning of the word *"mortuum"*[21] becomes very difficult to understand. This gloss stated that the canon in this case had reference not to the clergy but only to the laity. *("Laici, nam clerici mortui bene induuntur vestibus sacris."),* and that it was proper to bury the clergy in the sacred vestments. It seems that glossator misinterpreted this point, inasmuch as the canon itself made no distinction regarding the persons who were forbidden such burial. Apparently the glossator had in mind the vestments which the priest wore at Mass rather than the sacred vestments, the corporal and the altar cloths, as the canon itself seemed to indicate; the canon mentioned the *"altaris palla,"* while the gloss used the term *"vestis sacer."* Durandus, too, in discussing the altar vestments, mentioned the prohibition and stated that it was unlawful to bury people *"in pannis altaris."*[22]

A severe penalty was in store for those clerics who permitted the use of the altar vestments for burials or who considered it a matter of small or little importance. The penalty for the deacon who presumed to take such an attitude was a suspension of three years and six months; for the priest, the suspension was to last for ten years and five months; the reconciliation was to be made with

[19] C. 40, D. I, *de cons.;* this canon is likewise taken from the Letter of Clement to James, the Brother of the Lord; cf. *supra,* fn. 17.

[20] Cf. *glossae* s.v. *altaris palla* on c. 39, D. I, *de cons.,* and s.v. *nemo* on c. 40, D. I, de cons.

[21] Cf. *glossa* s.v. *mortuum* on c. 40, D. I, *de cons.*

[22] Cf. Durandus, *Rationale Divinorum Officiorum,* Lib. I, Cap. III, n. 50.

great humility.[23] It should be noted, however, that this penalty is not confirmed in any other section of the *Decree* of Gratian.

The sacred furnishings were to be used only for divine services. Their use for any other purpose was strictly prohibited. To quote the *Decree* itself: "They are not to enjoy any other uses than those which are becoming to ecclesiastical functions and to God.[24] The reason given in the canon was related to the great respect which the ancient Jews had for the sacred vessels; in particular it referred to the fate of Balthasar who dared to profane the sacred vessels of the Jews. This prescription is apparently very ancient; there was mention of it in the *Constitutiones Apostolorum* (Canon 72) which forbade the conversion of the sacred vessels into secular uses.

There was one possible exception to this law: it was permissible to melt down the sacred vessels and sell them for the purpose of helping the poor, and in particular for the ransoming of captives.[25]

Gratian's collection did not contain any prescriptions which dealt directly with the matter which concerned the need for or the minister of the blessing or consecration of the sacred furnishings. However, the point was mentioned indirectly in conjunction with other problems. Thus, it was forbidden to celebrate Mass or to offer sacrifices to God in any vessels other than those which had been blessed or consecrated by bishops.[26]

The canon which specified that the altar linens or sacred vestments were to be made of linen likewise contained the added prescription that these altar cloths were to be blessed by the bishops.[27] Again, the canon which dealt with the matter of who should or should not wear the sacred vestments likewise added that they were to be blessed.[28]

[23] C. 40, D. I, *de cons.*

[24] C. 42, D. I, *de cons.;* canon ascribed to the decretal letter of a Pope Stephen to a certain Hilary; cf. Jaffé K, n. 130; and Hinschius, p. 183.

[25] C. 70, C. XII, q. 2; canon taken from St. Ambrose, Liber III, *De Officiis;* cf. *Nicene and Post-Nicene Fathers of the Christian Church,* (2nd series, Vol. X, New York, 1896) Vol. X, St. Ambrose, *Select Works and Letters, Duties of the Clergy,* Bk. II, Chap. 28, n. 142, p. 65; *MPL,* XVI, 142.

[26] C. 2, D. I, *de cons.;* cf. *supra,* p. 4.

[27] C. 46, D. I, *de cons.*

[28] C. 42, D. I, *de cons.*

The matter of touching or handling the sacred vessels and vestments received considerable comment in the *Decree* of Gratian. In brief, it can be said that the law of the *Decree* was the same as is prevalent today, namely, that only clerics were allowed to handle the sacred vessels. Only consecrated persons, that is to say, clerics in major orders, were allowed to handle the sacred vessels and vestments.[29]

Women, all women without exception, even those who were consecrated to God, such as nuns, were absolutely forbidden to handle the sacred vessels and vestments.[30] In fact, the canon quoted the Holy See as using very harsh language with regard to such a practice, as commanding it to be stopped most speedily, and as adding further that this "*pestis*" was to be wiped out at once before it spread any further.

One canon forbade even subdeacons to touch the sacred vessels.[31] This, however, was somewhat contradicted in the canon which forbade the lectors to touch the sacred vessels. There it was stated that the lectors were not allowed to carry the sacred vessels, nor were any other persons to do so except those who had been ordained subdeacons by the bishops.[32]

The gloss on this canon attempted to explain away the discrepancy by saying that in this case what was meant by the sacred vessels were actually reliquaries.[33] In reality, the discrepancy more than likely arose because of the fact that these canons were written some two centuries apart and could not be said to belong to the age when the glossators were at work.

Canon 32, D. XXIII seemed to have quite definitely settled the

[29] C. 41, D. I, *de cons.;* canon taken from the Letter of Pope Sixtus to the Universal Church; spurious; cf. Jaffé K, n. 32; Hinschius, p. 108; cf. also c. 40, D. I, *de cons.;* and c. 30, D. XXIII; this last canon is authentic, having been taken from the Council of Agde (506); cf. Mansi, VIII, 335.

[30] C. 25, D. XXIII; canon attributed to Pope Sotherus in his Second Letter to the Bishops of Italy; spurious, cf. Jaffé K, n. 61, and Hinschius, p. 124.

[31] C. 26, D. XXIII; authentic canon from the Council of Laodicaea (343-381), cf. Mansi, II, 567.

[32] C. 31, D. XXIII; authentic canon from the I Council of Braga (563), cf. Mansi, IX, 778.

[33] Cf. *glossa* s.v. *non liceat portare* on c. 31, D. XXIII.

matter by stating very simply that deacons and even acolytes were allowed to touch the sacred vessels and vestments.[34]

The washing of the sacred vestments or linens was subject to many more regulations than is the case today. First of all, special basins were to be provided for this purpose; the sacred linens were to be washed in these basins to the exclusion of all other washings.[35] Moreover, each sacred linen was to be washed in a different basin; the corporals in one, the altar cloths in another, and the *vela ianuarum* in yet another.[36] This was a very ancient prescription, being found also in the *Ordo Romanus* of Hittorp.[37]

The deacons were the persons to whom the duty of washing the sacred linens was entrusted. This was a task which was to be done indoors, in the sacristy; in this, too, the deacons were to be assisted by the lesser ministers. It was considered sinful for any one to perform the washing in any other manner. The reason which was given for this law was to prevent any possible danger of profanation to those small particles, invisible to the naked eye, of the Body of Christ that might still have been adhering to the corporals.[38] It should be observed that no provision was made to have any other person than a deacon wash the linens even for the second or third washing. Rather, the whole tenor of the law seemed to indicate that no one who was not at least an acolyte was to touch the sacred linens.

There was also a particular regulation regarding the manner in which were to be washed those linens onto which the Precious Blood has been spilled. The minister was to wash such linens three times, and at the same time, i.e., during each washing, he was

[34] Authentic canon from *Capitula collecta a Martino Episcopo Bracarensi;* cf. Mansi, IX, 885; also A. Van Hove, *Prolegomena* (2 ed., Romae, H. Dessain, 1945), no. 268, pp. 278-279.

[35] C. 106, D. IV, *de cons.;* authentic canon from the Council of Lerida (524); cf. Mansi, IV, 476.

[36] C. 40, D. I, *de cons.*

[37] *Ordo Romanus* (cf. *supra*, p. 1) *Caput Clementis de Pallis;* this prescription is found in nearly all the manuscripts of the Ordines Romani; cf. Andrieu, *Les* Ordines Romani *du Haut Moyen Âge,* pp. 46, 121, 150, 159, 180, 217, 375, 390, 403, 424, 431.

[38] C. 40 D. I, *de cons.*

to hold the chalice under the spot being washed. Finally, he was to consume the ablution.[39]

The only notable conclusion to be observed from the study of the law on the sacred furnishings in the *Decree* of Gratian is that not one of the canons was derived from the general law. Those canons which were authentic were derived from particular councils; those which had some semblance of universality, i.e., as coming from the Holy See, were spurious, being derived for the most part from the pseudo-Isidorian Decretals.

[39] C. 27, D. II, *de cons.;* spurious canon, ascribed to a decretal of Pope Pius I; cf. Jaffé K, n. 52.

CHAPTER II

THE LAW ON THE SACRED FURNISHINGS IN THE DECRETALS

The remainder of the *Corpus Iuris Canonici* did not contain legislation on the sacred furnishings even as complete as that contained in Gratian. In fact, the glossators and commentators on the Decretals to a large extent referred back to Gratian for many of their explanations. In view of the fact, however, that none of the law in Gratian was based on any general authentic law, and that the Decretals are authentic law, it is thought helpful here to consider the legislation in the Decretals and Decretalists in two sections, namely that legislation which repeated the law as found in Gratian, and that legislation which was new or different from Gratian.

Article I: The Law of the Decretals Which Repeated the Law of Gratian Regarding the Sacred Furnishings

It may well be pointed out again that, although the term "sacred furnishings" *(Sacra Supellex)* did not appear in the Decretals, still nearly all of the sacred furnishings were known at the time of this collection. Thus one gloss pointed out that by the word *"cimilia"* were to be understood all the vessels of the Church.[1]

Again, in prescribing for the care of the Holy Eucharist, the legislator specifically mentioned practically all of the sacred furnishings: the vessels of the ministry, the vestments of the ministers, the altar cloths, the corporals, and the stoles.[2] One commentator pointed out that in this canon the law meant to include the oil stocks, the basins for washing the linens, especially the chalice, in the phrase "vessels of the ministry."[3]

[1] Cf. *glossa* s.v. *cimilia* on c. 3, X, *de officio Archdiaconi,* I, 23.

[2] C. 2, X, *de custodia Eucharistiae, chrismatis, et aliorum sacramentorum,* III, 44; taken from the IV General Council of the Lateran (1215), c. 20; cf. Mansi, XXII, 1007.

[3] Cardinalis Hostiensis (Henricus de Segusio), *Commentaria in Quinque*

Regarding the materials suitable for the manufacture of the sacred vessels, namely, the chalice and the paten, the Decretals treated of the matter only in an incidental manner. It was mentioned in the Decretal which ordered that the priest who had used a wooden chalice for the celebration of Mass should be deprived of his office and benefice.[4] Hence it is clear that wood was not to be used for chalices. When the gloss on this canon explained that the use of wooden chalices was forbidden, it employed the same reasons that the glossators of Gratian had used.[5]

The commentaries on this canon were more specific; they stated further that the chalice and the paten were not to be made of wood, glass, copper, or brass; rather, they should be made of gold or silver. They, too, used as their basis for such reasoning the canons and glosses thereon in the *Decree* of Gratian.[6]

In this connection it should be mentioned that the first direct statement regarding the sacred vessels appeared in the thirteenth century. It was contained in a letter of Innocent IV (1243-1254) which stated very clearly that priests were to use only gold, silver, or tin chalices; that the corporal was to be made of linen; and that the altar should be covered with clean vestments and altar cloths.[7]

The Decretals contained no direct legislation regarding the use of sacred furnishings. It was considered indirectly with regard

---

Decretalium Libros (5 vols., Venetiis, 1581), Vol. III, p. 172. (Hereafter this work will be referred to as *Commentaria*).

[4] C. 14, X, *de celebratione missarum et sacramento Eucharistiae, et divinis officiis,* III, 41; Letter of Honorius III to the Bishop of Brescia; cf. A. Potthast, *Regesta Pontificum Romanorum inde ab anno post Christum natum MCXCVIII ad annum MCCCIV* (2 vols., Berolini, 1874-1875) n. 7825 (hereafter referred to as Potthast).

[5] Cf. *glossa* s.v. *ligneo* on c. 14, X, *de cel. miss. etc.,* III, 41.

[6] Cf. Hostiensis, *Commentaria,* III, 167; Abbas Panormitanus, *Commentria in Quinque Libros Decretalium* (5 vols. in 7, Venetiis, 1588), VI 328. (Hereafter this work will be referred to as *Commentaria*). Cf. also *supra,* pp. 4-5.

[7] Innocentius IV, ep. "Sub Catholicae," 6 mart. 1254-*Codicis Iuris Canonici Fontes,* cura Emi Petri Card. Gasparri editi (9 vols., Romae [postea Civitate Vaticana]: Typis Polyglottis Vaticanis, 1923-1939) (Vols. VII-IX ed. curra et studio Emi Iustiniani, Card. Serédi). (Hereafter this work will be referred to as *Fontes*). For this reference, *Fontes,* n. 34.

to the disposal of those sacred furnishings which were no longer usable for divine worship. Thus, in one decretal, there was proposed a question whether it was permissible to convert a house of hospitality which was attached to a religious house into a secular dwelling. The answer was given that it was not to be turned over to secular uses. The reasons for the reply were stated as follows: such a house was to be considered to be something sacred, as were the vessels and other utensils which had been dedicated to religious worship by the priests. Such articles could not be lawfully turned over to secular or profane use; such was the sanction of ancient custom and of the Fathers.[8] The gloss on this canon referred back to the work of Gratian, which treated of this matter as already considered in an earlier part of this work.[9]

The commentaries, too, generally referred back to Gratian, reiterating his law that worn-out furnishings were to be burned. They were not to be converted to secular uses.[10]

The *Liber Sextus* restated the law on this matter in clearer terms. Rule 51 of the *Rules of Law* of Boniface VIII (1294-1303) stated that once something was dedicated to God, it was not again to be transferred to human uses.[11] The glosses on this rule gave examples of its meaning. Suppose that a chasuble or other church furnishing was made of golden cloth; that it was worn-out and could not any longer be used for divine services; though some of the pieces thereof were still usable; was it lawful to use such pieces to make burses for secular purposes? The answer was in the negative, since even the pieces were considered to have been consecrated to God, and hence it was deemed improper that anything at all should be made from them for the use of private individuals. Another example was: suppose that a bishop somehow had consecrated a chalice without the knowledge of the owner

[8] C. 4, X, *de religiosis domibus,* III, 36; Letter of Urban III (1185-1187) to the Bishop of Rimini; cf. Jaffé L, 9866.

[9] Cf. *glossa* s.v. *mundanis usibus* on c. 4, X, III, 36; also *supra* pp. 5-6.

[10] Cf. Panormitanus, *Commentaria,* VI°, cap. 3, 336; VI, p. 284; S. Raymundus de Pennafort, *Summa* (Veronae, 1744), p. 311; Hostiensis, *Commentaria,* III, cap. 4, *de religiosis domibus,* p. 136.

[11] Reg. 51, R. J., in VI°; "Semel Deo dicatum, non est ad usus humanos ulterius transferendum."

and even contrary to his will. The answer was that such a chalice, having been consecrated, could not be returned to its owner if he was not a cleric, but indeed the price thereof was to be returned to its owner.[12]

Restrictions regarding the persons who were or were not to touch or handle the sacred vestments and vessels were not specified in the Decretals themselves. The glossators and commentators, however, treated of the matter to some extent. They reiterated the law of Gratian to the effect that only consecrated persons, by whom were meant clerics in major orders, were to touch the sacred furnishings.[13]

It was considered so serious a matter that the gloss on the decretal which dealt with the matter concerning the vessels and vestments which had been used by schismatic priests pointed out that the entire doubt in the decretal had been raised by the fact that these furnishings had been used by unconsecrated persons.[14]

The Decretals did not mention the matter of washing the sacred linens. However, it is not out of place here to mention the observation of Thomassinus (1619-1695). He noted that the Council of Saumer (1253) in its third canon ordered that the corporals should be washed by a deacon or a priest vested in the sacred vestments; then those linens and the other sacred furnishings of the altar were to be washed by a pious virgin or by a matron whose life was above suspicion.[15]

This observation is worthy of note for the simple reason that for the first time mention was made of allowing some one other than a cleric to handle the sacred vestments, even if only for laundering purposes.

[12] Cf. glosses on Rule 51.

[13] Cf. *glossa* s.v. *sed pars illa* on 1, X, *de vita et Honestate Clericorum* III, 1.

[14] Cf. *glossa* s.v. *benedici* in c. 2, X, *de sacramentis non iterandis,* I, 16; cf. also Prosper Fagnanus, *Commentaria in Quinque Libros Decretalium* (5 vols. in 3, Venetiis, 1709-1729), I, cap. 12-13, pp. 445 sqq. (Hereafter this work will be referred to as Fagnanus).

[15] L. Thomassinus, *Vetus et Nova Ecclesiae Disciplina* (10 vols., Magontiaci, 1787) Pars I, Lib. 2, cap. 6, no. 2; cf. also Mansi XXIII, 809.

Article II: Development of the Law on the Sacred Furnishings in the Decretals

A few of the lacunae in the law of Gratian on the sacred furnishings were filled in particularly with respect to that part of the law that regarded the conservation and safekeeping of the sacred furnishings. This particular matter received more consideration than any other single point in the Decretals, that is to say, in so far as the sacred furnishings are concerned.

Reiterating the legislation of the IV General Council of the Lateran on the abuse or misuse of churches,[16] the Decretals severely condemned the practice of uncleanliness and carelessness which seemed to prevail in many churches of that day.[17]

This Decretal further commanded that these furnishings, stoles, vessels, corporals, and altar cloths, should be kept neat and clean. It went on to point out that it was absurd even to think that sacred things were cared for so poorly and remained so much neglected. Such carelessness and neglect would be disgusting and revolting even with regard to mundane things.

The *Clementinae* legislated against the same abuse, noting that in many churches the vessels, vestments, and other furnishings necessary for divine services were indecently kept; this abuse was to be corrected.[18]

Of more interest, although almost purely historical today, is the consideration of whose duty it was to safeguard the sacred furnishings and to keep them in decent repair. It should be noted at once that the law of the Decretals on this matter does not rightly belong to that period but rather to pre-Gratian times.

It appears that the officer in the church who was ultimately responsible in this matter was the archdeacon. This was to be expected inasmuch as in the Mediaeval Church he was the one

16 Cf. the IV General Council of the Lateran (1215), c. 20; Mansi, XXII, 1007.

17 C. 2, X, *de custodia Eucharistiae, chrismatis, etc.*, III, 14.

18 C. 1, *de celebratione missarum, et aliis divinis officiis*, III, 14, in Clem. Clement V, in the Council of Vienne (1311-1312).

who usually administered the temporalities of the church.[19] However, inasmuch as the archdeacon was a diocesan officer, his supervision was of a remote rather than a direct character.

The Decretals further indicated that the archdeacon did not perform this office personally, but rather delegated the duty to the sacristan *(sacrista)* and/or to the custodian *(custos)*. The chief duty of the sacristan was the care of the sacred furnishings, that is to say, the safeguarding of the sacred vessels, of the ecclesiastical vestments, and of the treasury of the church; he also had the care of the candles, of the oil, and of the distribution of the chrism. It must be observed that the canon specified that the sacristan was to act always under the supervision of the archdeacon.[20]

Another officer, the custodian, seemed to be charged with duties which were, for practical purposes, very nearly identical with those of the sacristan. It was his duty to safeguard assiduously the altar linens, and all the utensils of the church; (the glossator explained that here the term "utensils" was to be understood to mean particularly the sacred vessels).[21] In like manner, he was to be solicitous for all the ornaments of the church and to see to it that the candles or lamps were lighted and extinguished.[22]

The glossators as well as the commentators on these canons seemed to be somewhat confused at the idea that there should be two officers whose duties were apparently identical. The glossator observed that their duties were actually identical and that ultimately the duties of either or of each were determined by the custom peculiar to a particular place.[23] Hostiensis (d. 1271) con-

[19] C. 3, V, *de officio Archidiaconi,* I, 23. Letter of Gregory III to the Archdeacon of Salon; cf. Jaffé K, 722.

[20] C. 1, X, *de officio Sacristae* I, 26; the source of this canon is unknown; cf. *Corpus Iuris Canonici* (Ed. Lipsiensis secunda, post Aemilii Richteri curas . . . instruxit Aemilius Friedburg, 2 vols., Lipsiae, 1879-1881), Vol. II, p. XVIII.

[21] Cf. *glossa* s.v. *utensilia* on c. 1, X, *de officio custodis,* I, 27.

[22] C. 1, and 2, X, *de officio custodis,* I, 27; canons ascribed to the *Ordo Romanus* and the Council of Toledo; no such office can be found in the *Ordo Romanus;* the reference to the Council of Toledo is also uncertain; cf. *Corpus Iuris Canonici,* Vol. II, p. XVIII.

[23] Cf. *glossa* s.v. *sive in cera* in c. 1, X, *de officio Sacristae,* I, 26.

curred with the glossator in this opinion.[24] Fagnanus (1598-1678), on the contrary, apparently not having been able to reconcile himself to the idea of these two offices being the same, made a distinction: he excepted from the care of the custodian the safeguarding of the gold or silver vessels and of the precious vestments; these, he claimed, were to be looked after by the sacristan, whom he identified with the church treasurer *(thesauraurius)*.[25] His reasoning on the situation was based on the note in the *Margarita* to the *Decree* of Gratian, wherein the sacristan was identified as the treasurer.[26]

Returning again to the concept that the sacristan and the custodian were to perform their duties under the supervision of the archdeacon, one notes that the law was very specific, particularly with regard to the custodian. Rules were enunciated as to what was to be done about a custodian who proved himself to be inefficient. The archdeacon, first of all, was to urge the custodian to mend his ways. If this proved futile, and the custodian still did not perform his duties properly, the archdeacon was to denounce him to the bishop; and having removed anyone who was inefficient, he was to provide a capable custodian or minister of the House of God in his place.[27]

The decretal law placed a great deal of emphasis on the dignity of the office of the custodian. Though very likely the extolment of this office drew more heavily on symbolism than upon legal actuality, the custodian was esteemed as one of the three pillars of the church together with the archdeacon and the archpriest. He seemed to be placed on a par with the two latter officers; the three were expected to co-operate wholeheartedly without jealousy or envy.[28]

That a blessing or consecration was considered necessary for the sacred furnishings becomes more apparent when one considers that there was a law which required a re-blessing or a re-

[24] Cf. *Summa Aurea* (Basileae, 1573), p. 64.

[25] Fagnanus, I, cap. *de officio custodis,* p. 517.

[26] Cf. *supra,* p. 8.

[27] C. 1, X, *de officio custodis,* I, 27.

[28] C. 2, X, *de officio custodis,* I, 27.

consecration in the case of those furnishings which had become desecrated. Thus, in one decretal, it was asked whether vessels and vestments which had been used by schismatic priests were to be re-consecrated. The answer was in the negative.[29]

The commentaries and the gloss expanded on the cases when a re-blessing or a re-consecration might be necessary. Barbosa (1589-1649) stated that the consecration was lost and that another consecration was needed only when the form of the furnishing was entirely or seriously changed.[30]

The gloss on this particular decretal noted further that, in the repairing of the sacred vestments, patches could be added without having been blessed, and that the repaired garment was not in any need of another blessing.[31] No mention was made of cases of the profane or criminal use of the sacred furnishings. In general, the commentaries regarded the gloss as prescribing the proper procedure to be followed with regard to the blessings or consecrations which were needed when vestments were being or had been repaired.[32]

[29] C. 2, X, *de sacramentis non iterandis,* I, 16; Letter of Honorius III to the Archbishop of London; cf. Potthast, n. 1019.

[30] Augustinus Barbosa, *Iuris Ecclesiastici Libri Tres* (Lugduni, 1660), Liber Tertius, Cap. 2—*De vasis sacris, et vestibus, et aliis rebus sacris in communi,* p. 113. (Hereafter this work will be referred to as Barbosa.)

[31] Cf. *glossa* s.v. *consecrato* in c. 3, X, *de consecratione ecclesiae vel altaris,* III, 40.

[32] Cf. Fagnanus, III, p. 445; Hostiensis, *Commentaria,* III, Cap. *quod in dubiis,* p. 160.

PART TWO

SECTION ONE

PRESENT DAY LAW REGARDING THE SACRED FURNISHINGS

Introduction

At first glance, going directly from the law of the *Corpus Juris* to the current legislation regarding the sacred furnishings would seem to leave a considerable lacuna in the treatment of the law on this matter. However, the legislation regarding the sacred furnishings of churches, as is the case with most matters liturgical, began to take definite authoritative form after the Council of Trent.

While the Council itself did not legislate directly on the sacred furnishings, one resolution, namely the establishment of a commission for the revision of the Missal and Breviary,[1] had far-reaching effects on the present state of the liturgy and hence on the sacred furnishings. The period from the sixteenth century to the present is referred to as the period of the unified universal Roman liturgy under the authority of the Roman Pontiff.[2]

Among the chief sources of the present law are the liturgical books published as a result of the resolution of the Council of Trent mentioned above. These are the *Roman Missal,* approved by Pope Pius V (1566-1572) in 1570[3] (the first liturgical book to be prescribed for the entire Church of the Latin Rite); the *Roman Pontifical,* edited by Pope Clement VIII (1592-1605) in 1596;[4] the *Roman Ritual,* published by Pope Paul V (1605-1621) in 1614;[5] the *Ceremonial* of Bishops, produced in 1600 by Pope Clement VIII.[6]

[1] Conc. Trident., sess. XXII, *de sacrificio missae,* c. 5; can. 7.

[2] Cf. Callewaert, *Liturgicae Institutiones,* Tractatus Primus, *De S. Liturgia Universim* (ed. alt. Brugis; Beyaert, 1925), pp. 82-100.

[3] Pius V, const. *Quo primum tempore,* 14 iul. 1570—*Fontes,* n. 135.

[4] Clemens VIII, const. *Ex quo,* 10 febr. 1596—*Fontes,* n. 180.

[5] Paulus V, const. *Apostolicae Sedis,* 17 ian. 1614—*Fontes,* n. 198.

[6] Clemens VIII, litt. ap. *Cum novissime,* 14 iul. 1600—*Bullarum Diplomatum et Privilegiorum Sanctorum Romanorum Pontificum Taurinensis Editio* (24 vols. et Appendix, Augustae Taurinorum, 1857-1872), X, 597-598 (hereafter cited as *BRT*).

Another important, and in some respects the most important, factor in the development of the law on sacred furnishings was the establishment of the Sacred Congregation of Rites by Pope Sixtus V (1585-1590) in 1588 to watch over and enact new laws regarding the rites and ceremonies of the Church.[7] It is in the Collection of the Decrees of the Sacred Congregation of Rites[8] that one finds a great wealth of information regarding the law on sacred furnishings, particularly regarding the individual furnishings and interpretation of the rubrics of the liturgical books.

In addition to the above-mentioned source for the present-day law on the sacred furnishings there are several statements of the Sovereign Pontiff himself; these however are, for the most part, incorporated into the law of the Code itself.

The treatment of the law on the sacred furnishings in the Code of Canon Law, Title XVIII, canons 1296-1306, is largely of a general nature. Section One of this work, entitled the *Law Regarding the Sacred Furnishings in General,* will be a commentary on this part of the Code.

Section Two, *The Principal Sacred Furnishings in Particular,* will derive mainly from the Liturgical Books and the Decrees of the Congregation of Rites.

[7] Sixtus V, const. *Immensa,* 22 ian. 1588—*BRT,* VIII, 985-999.

[8] *Decreta Authentica Congregationis Sacrorum Rituum,* ex actis eiusdem collecta eiusque auctoritate promulgata sub auspiciis Ss. Domini Nostri Leonis Papae XIII. (7 vols., Vols. I-V, Romae, 1898-1901; Vol. VI, Appendix, sub auspiciis Pii Papae X, Romae, 1912; Vol. VII, Appendix, sub auspiciis Pii Papae XI, Romae, 1927). This collection will be cited as *Decr. Auth.*

SECTION ONE

LAW REGARDING THE SACRED FURNISHINGS IN GENERAL

CHAPTER III

MATERIAL AND FORM OF THE SACRED FURNISHINGS

Prior to the Code there do not appear to have been any general norms governing the material and form of the sacred furnishings. There were, it is true, treatises by some of the authors about sacred furnishings. St. Charles Borromeo, for example, treated of the sacred furnishings at great length; in fact, to our knowledge his is the most complete and detailed work on the matter to date.[1] This is such a complete treatise that it is difficult to understand why more authors did not use him as a source.[2]

Other authors who wrote before the Code also have treatises on the sacred furnishings.[3] However, none of them ventured to set forth a general norm, such as is now found in the Code, that regarding the material and form of the sacred furnishings one should observe the laws of the liturgy, ecclesiastical tradition and, in so far as it is possible, the laws of sacred art.[4]

[1] *Acta Ecclesiae Mediolanensis,* cura et studio A. Ratti (3 vols. in 2, Mediolani, 1890-1892). *Instructionum Supellectilis Ecclesiasticae Liber II,* Vol. II, columns 1503-1588. Also *Regulae et Instructiones de Nitore et Munditia Ecclesiarum, Altarium, Sacrorum Locorum, et Supellectilis Ecclesiasticae,* Vol. II, columns 1589-1598. (Hereafter this work will be cited as *Acta Eccl. Mediol.*).

[2] Aloysius Adone, *Synopsis Canonico-Liturgica* (Neapoli, 1886) (hereafter cited as Adone) and B. Gavantus, *Thesaurus Sacrorum Ritum* (Venetiis, 1672) (hereafter cited as Gavantus), appear to be the only authors to have used the work of St. Charles Borromeo.

[3] Cf. F. X. Wernz, *Ius Decretalium* (6 vols., Vol. III, 2, ed., Romae et Prati, 1908), III, nn. 501 sqq. Petrus Gasparri, *Tractatus Canonicus de Sanctissima Eucharistia* (2 vols., Parisiis, 1897) (hereafter cited as *De SS Eucharistia*) Cap. V, *De Sacris Utensilibus,* nn. 653 sqq.

[4] Canon 1296, §3.

One should not encounter any difficulty in following the laws of the liturgy. These are found in the liturgical books and in the Decrees of the Sacred Congregation of Rites. It is not the province of this work to discuss the binding force of the rubrics of the liturgical books. It suffices to point out that the Code itself states that generally it does not legislate regarding the liturgical precepts, and that these retain their binding force unless the Code expressly corrects them.[5] Furthermore, Pope Pius XII, in his encyclical letter on the Sacred Liturgy, says the following regarding the observance of liturgical precepts:

> First of all, you must strive that with due reverence and faith all obey the decrees of the Council of Trent, of the Roman Pontiffs, and the Sacred Congregation of Rites, and what the liturgical books ordain concerning external public worship.[6]

Ecclesiastical tradition and the laws of sacred art remain somewhat difficult to analyze and even more difficult to define. The cardinal principle is: always bear in mind that these things are to be used in the worship of God. What has been stated regarding the art of the entire church edifice can well be restated regarding the sacred furnishings:

> A Catholic Church is a temple wherein the divine mysteries are celebrated and perpetuated. Its center, its culminating point, is the altar. The whole and all its parts converge toward this divine and human center, toward Him who is there: *Magister adest.* All other considerations, however ingenious they may be, considerations of structure, of originality, of sturdiness, or of delicacy must be subordinated to the dominant thought which the artist must have of the Eucharistic realities.[7]

Likewise, the three characteristics which the Sovereign Pontiff says should adorn all liturgical services may well be predicated

[5] Canon 2.

[6] Pius XII, litt. encycl. *Mediator Dei,* 20 nov. 1947, #187. (Translation used is the Vatican Library Translation edited by the National Catholic Welfare Conference, Washington, D. C.)

[7] E. Roulin, *Modern Church Architecture,* (St. Louis, Mo., and London: Herder Book Co., 1947), pp. 132-133.

of the sacred furnishings: "sacredness, which abhors any profane influence; nobility, which true and genuine arts should serve and foster: and universality, which, while safeguarding local and legitimate custom, reveals the catholic unity of the Church."[8]

This gives the key to the constant tenor of recent Pontifical pronouncements on sacred art. The guide to be followed is: we are dealing with something sacred, something which is to be used in the official public worship of the Church. Hence the objective is that of fostering devotion on the part of the faithful. If what is employed detracts from that devotion, it has no place in the liturgy and cannot be called sacred art.

Thus in an address on the occasion of the dedication of the new Vatican Picture Gallery on October 27, 1932, the Sovereign Pontiff condemned the so-called "New Sacred Art" as "unmoral" and therefore unworthy to have part in the building or decoration of the house of God and of prayer. He pointed out further that "bishops are to watch . . . that nothing be permitted under the false name of art to offend against the sanctity of the church and the altar, and to disturb the piety of the faithful."[9]

From this statement of the Holy Father one might be led to conclude that any departure from the traditional style in art is to be condemned. However, the real norm appears to lie not so much in such a departure but rather in the statement that nothing be permitted to "offend against the sanctity of the church, and the altar, and disturb the piety of the faithful."

In fact, the latest encyclical on the liturgy condemns excessive archaism as a norm.

> Just as obviously unwise and mistaken is the zeal of one who in matters liturgical would go back to the rites and usage of antiquity, discarding the new patterns introduced by disposition of divine Providence to meet the change of circumstances and situation.[10]

---

[8] Encycl. *Mediator Dei,* n. 188.

[9] *Acta Apostolicae Sedis, Commentarium Officiale* (Romae, 1909-), XXIV (1932), 356-357 (hereafter referred to as *AAS*).

[10] Encycl. *Mediator Dei,* n. 63.

This is further borne out in several recent pronouncements wherein the Sacred Congregation for the Propagation of the Faith encouraged native art. Thus, for example, upon the presentation to His Holiness Pope Pius XI of an exhibit of sacred pictures done in Japanese style, the Holy Father expressed great satisfaction, and the Cardinal Prefect of the Sacred Congregation for the Propagation of the Faith wrote to the Apostolic Delegate of Japan:

> An art which is at once thoroughly Catholic and distinctly national will be a concrete and effective proof that the Church is not identified with or bound to any particular form of culture, but that she welcomes whatever she finds that is good and beautiful in all peoples.[11]

The Cardinal Prefect of the same Congregation expressed these sentiments still more clearly in a letter to the Apostolic Delegate of the Belgian Congo. In this letter he pointed out that "in the making of articles of devotion a careful account is to be taken of the lines, the colors, and all the elements native to the Congo art."[12]

For all of this encouragement of native art, which is certainly foreign to the Western mind, the Church still seems to follow a middle course. Its comment regarding the introduction of Gothic Vestments was that such changes, "being contrary to the approved practice of the Church, can often cause disturbance and produce astonishment in the minds of the faithful."[13]

Pope Pius XII emphasizes the need to follow the middle course:

> Recent works of art which lend themselves to the materials of modern composition, should not be universally despised and rejected through prejudice. Modern art should be given free scope in the due and reverent service of the Church and the sacred rites, provided that they

[11] S. C. Prop. Fide., Letter, June 1, 1935. *Sylloge praecipuorum documentorum recentium Summorum Pontificum et S. Congregationis de Propaganda Fide necnon aliarum SS. Congregationum Romanorum ad usum missionariorum* (Civitate Vaticana; Typis Polyglottis Vaticanis, 1939). (Hereafter this work will be cited as *Sylloge.*) For this reference, *Sylloge,* n. 193.

[12] S.C. Prop. Fide., Letter, Dec. 14, 1936—*Sylloge,* n. 203 bis. Letters to the Apostolic Delegates of the East Indies and of China expressed the same idea; cf. *Sylloge,* n. 188 and 169 bis.

[13] *Decr. Auth.,* n. 4398; cf. pp.

preserve a correct balance to excessive "symbolism" and that the needs of the Christian community are taken into consideration rather than the particular taste or talent of the individual artist. Thus modern art will be able to join its voice to that wonderful choir of praise to which have contributed, in honor of the Catholic faith, the greatest artists throughout the centuries. Nevertheless, in keeping with the duty of Our office, We cannot help deploring and condemning those works of art, recently introduced by some, which seem to be a distortion and perversion of true art and which at times openly shock Christian taste, modesty and devotion, and shamefully offend the true religious sense. These must be entirely excluded and banished from our churches, like "anything else that is not in keeping with the sanctity of the place."[14]

---

[14] Encyl. *Mediator Dei,* no. 195.

CHAPTER IV

CARE AND PRESERVATION OF THE SACRED FURNISHINGS

ARTICLE I: CLEANLINESS AND NEATNESS DEMANDED BY THE LAW

It appears odd that any law should be necessary regarding the care and preservation of the sacred furnishings. That such furnishings should be kept neat, clean, and in good repair follows from their very nature as something sacred. Hence it can be said that the care and preservation of them is a corollary of the divine law, namely, that respect and reverence are due to sacred things.

Nonetheless, it is clear that the Church has found it necessary, in a way has been forced, to issue legislation on the matter because of the negligence of individuals, which negligence at times was apparently quite widespread. The Church's legislative solicitude for a proper concern about the sacred furnishings dates back to the Fourth General Council of the Lateran (1215),[1] when, as it will be recalled, serious invectives were directed against abuses on this score. Succeeding Sovereign Pontiffs called repeated attention to the prescription that linens should be kept clean and vestments in proper repair.[2] As late as the year 1775, however, it appears that abuses were still rampant in this regard. At any rate, on Christmas Day of that year, Pope Pius VI (1775-1799) directed to all ordinaries an encyclical letter which contained a most excoriating denunciation of those who were guilty of carelessness in this regard.

> Quam absonum esset episcopi domum mundiorem esse, et elegantius ornatam, quam sit sacrificii domus, sanctitatis hospitium, aula Dei vivi? Quam absurdum sacras vestes, altarium ornamenta, atque universalem supellectilem, vel vetustate squallentem, et conscissam, vel sordi-

---

[1] Cf. *supra* p. 2.

[2] Innocentius IV, ep. *Sub catholicae,* 6 mart. 1254, §3, n. 13—*Fontes,* n. 34; Benedictus XIV, const. *Etsi Pastoralis,* 26 maii 1742, §VI, n. XX—*Fontes,* n. 328.

> bus foedatam intueri; mensam autem episcopi splendide paratam, sacerdotis indumenta nitidissima, et ad multam venustatem composita? *Quantae confusionis opprobrium est,* ut praeclare scripsit S. Petrus Damiani, *quod nonnulli in squallido linteo Dominicum corpus et offerant, et involvant, et quod non dignaretur potens quilibet, qui tamen vermis est, propriis adhibere labiis, in hoc isti corpus non verentur impornere Salvatoris.*[3]

As Gasparri commented on this passage, those who act in such wise give evident argument that their faith is very weak and that they have no love for the Lord hidden under the sacramental species.[4]

The present law, as contained in the Code, is a concise restatement of the former pronouncements on the care and preservation of the sacred furnishings. It states that sacred furnishings, particularly those which are consecrated or blessed in accordance with liturgical laws, and which are used for public worship, are to be carefully preserved in the sacristy of the church, or in some other place which is safe and becoming; and they are not to be used for profane purposes.[5]

Although the Code itself does not go into detail regarding the neatness, the cleanliness, and the condition of the sacred furnishings, these matters can be deduced particularly from the law as found in the liturgical books. Of utmost consideration is the statement of canon 1150, that the things which are consecrated or blessed with a constitutive blessing be treated with reverence *(reverenter tractentur)*. This reverence most certainly postulates that the sacred furnishings, at least those which have such a consecration or blessing, should be kept neat, clean, and in good repair.

The Liturgical books are most explicit. The *Roman Missal,* while not devoting any particular section to the consideration of the law on this matter, nonetheless makes mention that the vestments are not to be ragged or torn, but that they are to be in good repair, invitingly clean, and beautiful.[6] The corporal is expected to be clean.[7]

[3] Pius VI, encycl. *Inscrutabile,* 25 dec. 1775, §5—*Fontes,* n. 470.

[4] *De Sanctissima Eucharistia,* n. 664.

[5] Canon 1296, §1.

[6] *Missale Romanum,* ex decreto Sacrosancti Concilii Tridentini restitutum,

The statement of the law in the *Roman Ritual* is still more precise: the responsible priest shall see to it that the sacred furnishings, vestments, vessels, ornaments, linens, and the vessels of the ministry are in good repair, neat, and clean.[8]

The *Ceremonial of Bishops* prescribes that the sacristan see to it, as his chief duty, that the sacred vestments, vessels, books, candles, ornaments and instruments for the use of the church and the altars be preserved whole, entire, and clean; and that when they become torn or ragged they be repaired or replaced.[9]

It is very manifest that the present law demands the giving of a most meticulous attention to the neatness, cleanliness, and preservation of the sacred furnishings. A practical guide for the proper upkeep of these furnishings can be found in the work of St. Charles Borromeo: *Regulae et Instructiones de Nitore et Munditia Ecclesiarum, Altarium, Sacrorum Locorum, et Supellectilis Ecclesiasticae.*[10]

Article 2: The Proper Place for Storing the Sacred Furnishings

The Code prescribes the sacristy as the proper storage place for the sacred furnishings. This is to be expected inasmuch as the very

---

S. Pii V. Pontificis Maximi iussu editum, aliorum Pontificum cura recognitum, a Pio X reformatum, et Benedicti XV auctoritate vulgatum. (Editio III iuxta typicam Vaticanam, Neo Eboraci: Benziger Brothers, 1944 (hereafter cited as *Missale Romanum*), Tit. *Ritus servandus in celebratione missae,* n. 2.

7 Ibid., tit. *De Defectibus in ministerio ipso occurentibus,* n. 1.

8 "Curabit etiam, ut sacra supellex, vestes, ornamenta, linteamina, et vasa ministerii integra, nitidaque sint et munda."—*Rituale Romanum,* Pauli V Pontificis Maximi iussu editum, aliorumque Pontificum cura recognitum atque auctoritate Pii Pape XI ad normam Codicis Iuris Canonici accommodatum. (Editio iuxta typicam Vaticanam (Novi Eboraci: Benziger Brothers, 1944.) Titulus I, Caput Unicum, *De ïis quae in administratione sacramentorum generaliter servanda sunt,* n. 9.

9 *Caeremoniale Episcoporum,* Clementis VIII, Innocentii X, et Benedicti XIII iussu editum, Benedicti XIV et Leonis XIII auctoritate recognitum (editio tertia post typicam. Taurini: Marietti, 1948.) Liber 1, cap. VI, n. 2.

10 *Acta Eccl. Mediol.,* Vol. II, col. 1589-1598.

term "sacristy," as defined by St. Charles Borromeo, is the place where the sacred furnishings are stored.[11] In consideration of what has been said concerning the neatness, cleanliness and preservation of the sacred furnishings, it is evident that the legislator is concerned with a safe and decent place for the storing of them. Hence, what is of paramount importance legally is that the appointments of the sacristy be so arranged as to guarantee both a decent and a careful storage for such furnishings as are not continually to be left on the altar or in the church, as well as a safe storage. The practice followed in many churches, namely of having a safe or a vault in the sacristy in which particularly the sacred vessels are stored, appears to be in complete harmony with the present law.

The fact that the Code mentions "some other safe and proper place" for storing the sacred furnishings probably has its root in two needs. First, churches constructed before the fifteenth century were not provided with sacristies.[12] Thence arose the need of some other place for the storing of the liturgical accessories. Secondly, not all modern churches are provided with a safe or a vault as mentioned above; hence the need for some other place which would be safe against the theft of particularly the sacred vessels and other more precious furnishings.

An excellent treatise on the construction and appointments of the sacristy can be found in the work *Churches, Their Plan and Furnishing.* This work goes into detail about the sacristy requirements for large and small churches, the types of chests and cupboards to be desired together with the proper dimensions thereof, the safe, etc.[13]

Article 3: Proper Use of the Sacred Furnishings

The last part of canon 1296, §1, states that the sacred furnishings are not to be used for profane purposes. As is evident from

[11] *Acta Eccl. Mediol., Instructionum Fabricae Ecclesiasticae Libri II,* Vol. II, col. 1473.

[12] Cf. Roulin, *Modern Church Architecture,* p. 231.

[13] Peter F. Anson, *Churches, Their Plan and Furnishing* (Milwaukee: Bruce, 1948). (Hereafter cited as *Churches.*) Chapter XVI, *The Sacristy,* pp. 172-177.

the use of the word *"praesertim"* earlier in the canon, a distinction is being made between what are called sacred furnishings in the strict sense and sacred furnishings in the broad sense. The canon appears to be dealing with sacred furnishings as considered in the strict sense; it specifically mentions that it is concerned about those furnishings which are consecrated or blessed for use in public worship in accordance with the liturgical laws.

There is another category of sacred furnishings, namely such as are not consecrated or blessed, at least not with a blessing required by the laws of the liturgy; such for example are the candlesticks, cruets, finger towels, purificators, etc.; this category is referred to as sacred furnishings in the broad sense.[14]

The profane use of sacred furnishings in the strict sense is prohibited by canon 1296, §1. The profane use of such furnishings is also prohibited by canon 1150 which states that things which are consecrated or blessed with a constitutive blessing are not to be used for profane purposes or for purposes other than those for which they were intended in virtue of such a consecration or blessing.

A constitutive blessing is one whereby a thing is divorced from its original or pristine and profane use and dedicated perpetually to divine worship.[15] Sacred furnishings in the strict sense are sacred precisely because they have been consecrated or blessed with a constitutive blessing as required by the laws of the liturgy. Hence, one must conclude that it would be contrary to the law to use the furnishings of this category for profane purposes.[16]

These furnishings are likewise not to be used for purposes other than those for which they are intended. The authors generally

[14] Cf. Wernz-Vidal, *Ius Canonicum ad normam Codicis Iuris exactum* (7 vols. in 8, Romae, apud Aedes Universitatis Gregorianae, 1923-1938) (hereafter cited as *Ius Canonicum*), Tom. IV, vol. 1, n. 415. Coronata, *Institutiones Iuris Canonici* (editio altera, 5 vols., Taurini-Romae: Marietti, 1939-1947) (hereafter cited as *Inst. Iur. Can.*), II, n. 976. Vermeersch-Creusen, *Epitome Iuris Canonici* (ed. 6a, 3 vols., Mechliniae-Romae: H. Dessain, 1937-1946) (hereafter cited as *Epitome* II), n. 623.

[15] Cf. Wernz-Vidal, *Ius Canonicum,* Tom. IV, vol. 1, n. 308.

[16] Canon 1497, §2; 1537.

forego comment on this latter point, and it is rather difficult to envisage examples of such a misuse. There was issued, however, a Decree that forbade the use of the burse for the collecting of alms.[17]

It appears that in general the interpretation of the rule of law that, "once something has been dedicated to God, it is not again to be transferred to human uses,"[18] has become considerably less severe than it was at the time of the *Corpus Iuris Canonici.*[19]

There is complete doctrinal agreement regarding the prohibited profane use of those things which are consecrated; the profane use of such articles, e.g., of a chalice employed in a theatrical performance, is considered grave sacrilege.[20]

Although the law itself does not distinguish between consecrated and blessed furnishings in the matter of their profane use, the commentators appear to be of the opinion that the profane use of articles which have not been consecrated but which have been blessed with a constitutive blessing is indeed illicit, but not seriously so. The examples commonly given are: the use of holy water to quench one's thirst or for cooking purposes; the use of blessed candles for common illumination. Such actions, it is said, are illicit, but they are not to be considered either as sacrilegious or even as seriously sinful. Further comment indicates that profane uses of such articles can easily become illicit if there is a just cause, provided of course that these uses be not sordid or do not involve any contempt for sacred things.[21] It may well be that these examples are not *a propos;* at least one author contends that the

[17] S.R.C., 2 maii 1919 *Decr. Auth,* n. 4354.

[18] Reg. 51, R.J., in VI: "Semel Deo dicatum non est ad usus humanos ulterius transferendum."

[19] Cf. *supra,* p. 18.

[20] Cf. Coronata, *Inst. Iur. Can.,* II, n. 877; Vermeersch-Creusen, *Epitome,* II, n. 625; Gasparri, *De SS Eucharistia,* n. 663. Cappello seems to dissent in saying "culpa hac in re levis per se est." Cf. Cappello, *Tractatus Canonico-Moralis De Sacramentis* (5 vols., Romae: Marietti. Vol. I, ed. 4a, 1945; II, ed. 4a, 1944, III, ed. alt., 1942; IV, ed. alt. 1947; V, ed. 5a, 1947) (hereafter cited as *De Sacramentis*), I, n. 106.

[21] Cf. Vermeersch-Creusen, *Epitome,* II, n. 468; Coronata, *Inst. Iur. Can.,* II, 877; Cappello, *De Sacramentis,* I, n. 106.

blessings imparted to candles and holy water are not constitutive, but rather invocative.[22]

In accord with this mitigated interpretation of Rule 51, modern authors concur that there can be used for profane purposes those sacred furnishings which have lost their blessing or consecration according to the provisions of canon 1305, §1, 1°, that is to say, because they have suffered so much damage or change that they have lost their original form and are no longer fit for the purpose to which they were dedicated. Thus, for example, using the parts or pieces of worn out chasubles to make burses for other purposes—something that had been forbidden under the law of the *Corpus Iuris Canonici,*[23] is now considered legitimate.[24]

This opinion appears to be wholly in accord with the present law. If an article loses its consecration or blessing according to the conditions contemplated in canon 1305, §1, 1°; then it no longer is sacred and can be treated as any other non-sacred or profane thing. Furthermore, it seems juridically logical to conclude (although the authors forego mentioning such a conclusion) that, even if an article lost its consecration or blessing in consequence of some sordid use or exposition to public sale, as mentioned in canon 1305, §1, 2°; there would no longer be applicable the prohibition mentioned in canons 1150 and 1296, §1, that is to say, when sacred furnishings in the strict sense have lost their consecration or blessing they no longer are sacred and can be treated as ordinary articles, as long as one can at the same time prescind from the presence of any and all contempt and scandal.

The profane use of non-sacred sacred furnishings, i.e., of sacred furnishings in the broad sense, seems likewise to be forbidden by the law. Canon 1296, §1, uses the word "especially" or "particu-

22 Regatillo, *Ius Sacramentarium* (2 vols., Santander: Sal Terrae, 1945-1946), II, n. 682.

23 Cf. *supra,* p. 18.

24 Cf. Vermeersch-Creusen, *Epitome,* II, n. 625; Coronata, *Inst. Iur. Can.,* II, n. 877. Sipos, *Enchiridion Iuris Canonici* (ed. 3a, Pécas; Ex Typographia "Haladás R. T.," 1936), p. 713; Gennari, *Consultazioni morali, canoniche, liturgiche* (Napoli, 1893), Cons. XXXIII. pp, 483-487. This last work is cited as the principal basis for their opinion by modern authors.

larly"[25] not in an exclusive but rather in an inclusive sense; hence the profane use of even non-sacred sacred furnishings appears to be prohibited.[26]

The prohibition of the profane use of non-sacred furnishings is apparently based on a reason different from that which was the basis for the prohibition of the profane use of sacred furnishings in the strict sense; non-consecrated or non-blessed furnishings are not in reality sacred, although one may think of them as possessing a quasi-sacredness in view of their use or destination for use in public worship. The prohibition of the profane use of these furnishings derives from the fact that none of the things employed in public worship should ever leave room for ridicule or contempt. However, it seems on occasion readily allowable to enlist in a profane use this category of furnishings.[27]

Ordinarily the sale of sacred furnishings is not illegal nor does it imply simony, unless, of course, a charge were added for this consecration or the blessing.[28] However, it appears to be legitimate to add a charge for the expenses involved in having the article consecrated or blessed.[29]

Another matter touching on the respect for the sacred furnishings is the disposal of them after they are no longer fit for use. This is a problem with which, strangely, modern authors do not concern themselves. It is odd, too, that either during the past or in the present no legislation has been enacted since the original appearance of a spurious canon as incorporated in the *Decree* of Gratian.[30]

Although it is true that sacred furnishings, when worn or damaged to such an extent that they no longer retain their pristine

[25] "Praesertim."

[26] Cf. Coronata, *Inst. Iur. Can.*, II, n. 877; Vermeersch-Creusen, *Epitome*, II, n. 625; Gasparri, *De Sanctissima Eucharistia*, n. 663.

[27] Coronata, *Inst. Iur. Can.*, II, n. 877; Vermeersch-Creusen, *Epitome*, II, n. 625.

[28] Canon 730.

[29] Coronata, *Inst. Iur. Can.*, II, 877. With reference to the sale of sacred furnishings, the concept of a public sale as envisaged by canon 1305 will be treated in Chapter VII, p. 88.

[30] Cf. *supra*, p. 8 and p. 17.

form, lose their consecration or blessing,[31] they nevertheless call for reverential treatment.[32] Furthermore, it sometimes happens that furnishings, though worn, do not lose their original form, but are nonetheless unsuitable for divine service because of their age or condition. Other furnishings, while neither being worn nor losing their original shape, simply fall into desuetude because of the exigencies of style.

Regarding all the furnishings that can be included under this category, one may quite legitimately ask the question: What is to be done with them? Several lines of procedure are permissible:

a) it is advisable to have them repaired if that is at all possible; b) they can be converted into other sacred utensils, e.g. a chalice or a paten could be made into a pyx; stoles could be made from chasubles; corporals, palls, and other small linens could be made from albs; c) the materials of such furnishings could be sold; however, all care should be exercised against the possible emergence of ridicule or of contempt; and d) the materials may be subjected to a complete destruction.[33]

Article 4: The Inventory of Sacred Furnishings

To further guarantee the safekeeping of the sacred furnishings, the law specifies that a complete inventory thereof be constructed and accurately kept up to date.[34] This inventory, as canon 1296 indicates, is to form a part of the universal inventory of all the assets of the church.[35] However, inasmuch as the sacred furnishings are such a large and important part of these assets, both from the viewpoint of their sacredness and of their need for divine services, not to mention their value in some instances, the inven-

[31] Canon 1305, §1, 1°.

[32] Cf. *supra*, pp. 16-18.

[33] Cf. Gasparri, *De SS. Eucharistia*, n. 680.

[34] Canon 1296, §2.

[35] Cf. Deviny, "Church Accounting and Finance," *The Ecclesiastical Review* (from 1889: *The American Ecclesiastical Review*, Vols. I-XXXII, Philadelphia, 1889-1905; from 1905: *The Ecclesiastical Review*, Vols. XXXIII-CIX, Philadelphia, 1905-1943; from 1944, *The American Ecclesiastical Review*, Washington, D. C., Vol. CX, 1944—), LXXI (1924) 266 (hereafter cited as *AER* and *ER* respectively).

tory thereof should most certainly form a distinct part of the total inventory.[36]

The inventory must be specific and accurate.[37] It should contain the following entries: a description of each furnishing; the condition of the furnishing; the initial purchase price of the furnishing; the present estimated value thereof. Moreover, as the law indicates, any changes in the furnishings, whether they be additions or deletions, are to be noted in the inventory.

The inventory is to be made out in duplicate, one copy to be kept in the archives of the administration, the other in the chancery office.[38] In like manner, all annotations are to be incorporated in each of the copies of the inventory. It is suggested by some that the local ordinaries legislate on the matter of the inventory.[39] In at least one instance in the United States, particular legislation specifies that the inventory is to be reviewed once a year, and that all the additions and revision are to be duly noted in the inventory as drawn up.[40]

The obligation of constructing the inventory of sacred furnishings is incumbent upon all churches and oratories, even private. This follows from the fact that the sacred furnishings are by their very nature dedicated to divine service; hence, they no longer have place in the open market or in profane situations and are subject to the authority of the Church. It seems perfectly to be within the competency of the ordinary to legislate on this matter.[41]

Canon 1522, 2° and 3°, appears to have in mind the administrators of churches or of pious institutions as the persons whose duty it is to construct the inventory. In the United States, the administrator of a church is usually the pastor. In such cases this duty is incumbent upon the pastor.[42] In other cases, the duty falls to

[36] Cf. Vromant, *De Bonis Ecclesiae Temporalibus* (Paris, 1927) n. 202.

[37] Canon 1522, 3°.

[38] Canon 1522, 3°.

[39] Vromant, *op. cit.*, n. 202; Coronata, *Inst. Iur. Can.*, II, n. 879.

[40] *Acta et Decreta Concilii Provincialis Portlandensis in Oregon IV Anno 1932,* (Portland, Ore., 1934), Statutum 145, 7°.

[41] Coronata, *op. cit.*, II, n. 879.

[42] Cf. *Acta et Decreta Concilii Provincialis Portlandensis in Oregon IV, loc. cit.*

those who are the administrators of the church or the oratory either by law or by the appointment of the ordinary. This is a legally logical conclusion from canon 1302, which specifies that the duty of caring for the sacred furnishings is incumbent upon the rectors of churches or upon such others to whom their care has been entrusted.

Article 5: Persons Responsible for the Conservation and Preservation of the Sacred Furnishings

Canon 1302 placed the responsibility for the care and preservation of the sacred furnishings upon the rectors of churches or upon those to whom the care thereof has been entrusted. In the administrative structure of the Church in the United States today this responsibility devolves upon the pastor. This is a change from the law of the *Corpus Iuris,* which presupposed the officer designated as sacristan or the custodian.[43]

The *Ceremonial of Bishops* still speaks of the office of sacristan as being necessary in a cathedral or collegiate church. His chief duty is the care and preservation of the sacred furnishings. He is to be a priest who has been selected with a view to his capabilities for this office; and, if need be, he is to be given assistants to help him perform the duties of his office properly.[44]

The office of sacristan in this sense is non-existent in American churches. However, Gasparri pointed out that today the sacristan of the *Corpus Iuris* is called the major sacristan, while the custodian is designated as the minor sacristan. In the lesser churches, i.e., other than cathedral or collegiate, the pastor or the rector is the major sacristan. Hence the duty of caring for the sacred furnishings devolves upon the pastor.[45]

Furthermore, the *Roman Ritual,* in its introductory chapter wherein it treats about the rules which are generally to be observed in the administration of the sacraments, places this responsibility upon the pastor or any other priest to whom the administration

[43] Cf. *supra,* pp. 21-23.

[44] *Caeremoniale Episcoporum,* Lib. I, cap. 6, nn. 1-2.

[45] *De SS, Eucharistia,* n. 666.

thereof pertains.[46] By one of these norms he is advised to see to it that the sacred furnishings are kept neat and clean.[47]

From these arguments it is quite manifest that in general the duty of the preservation and conservation of the sacred furnishings is incumbent upon the pastor. Some ordinaries have specifically placed the duty on the pastor by local legislation.[48] Hence, even though the actual care of the sacred furnishings may be delegated, as it frequently is, to the Altar Society, to a Sister Sacristan, or to some other person or persons, the legal responsibility for the conservation and preservation of these furnishings of the Church is still among the pastor's duties.

Article 6: Provision of the Sacred Furnishings

The law of the Code specifies that, unless other arrangements exist, those persons who in virtue of canon 1186 have the duty to repair the church have also the duty of seeing that sacred furnishings are provided.[49] Canon 1186 stated that the onus of repairing the church devolves first of all upon the funds of the church.[50] This appears to be a redundancy in the law: canon 1297 in pointing to canon 1186 expects that provision of the sacred furnishings be made from the funds of the church; on the other hand, the sacred furnishings themselves are part and parcel of the funds that service the purpose of divine worship of the church.

[46] *Rituale Romanum,* Tit. I, cap. 1, no. 3.

[47] *Ibid.* n. 9.

[48] *Synodus Dioecesana Fargensis Prima* (Milwaukee: Bruce, 1941), Statuta 476 et 480. *Acta et Decreta Concilii Provincialis Portlandensis in Oregon IV,* Decreta 215, 145, 7.

[49] Canon 1297.

[50] "Funds of the church" is here used in translation of the Latin *"bona fabricae."* The term is difficult to grasp in English. *"Fabrica"* is the church considered as a moral person. Cf. Wernz-Vidal, *Ius Canonicum,* Tom. IV, vol. 2, nn. 775-776. The "bona fabricae," then, are the goods of the church, or the sum total of its real and personal and property rights. Cf. Woywood, *A Practical Commentary on the Code of Canon Law* (10th printing, 2 vols., New York: Joseph F. Wagner, 1946), II, n. 1222. As others put it, they are constituted of whatever proceeds are destined for the repair of the church or for the conduct of divine worship therein. Cf. Vermeersch-Creusen, *Epitome,* II, n. 493.

Accordingly it seems that if there exist any funds that are not ear-marked for some set purpose, these funds of the church must serve whatever claims may arise in the providing of the sacred furnishings for the church.[51]

If such funds are totally lacking, the responsibility for providing the sacred furnishings devolves as follows: in the cathedral church, upon the bishop and the canons in proportion to their salaries, but not inclusive of that portion of their salaries that is necessary for their proper maintenance; next, upon the people of the diocese. One very wise decision suggests that those who cannot afford money volunteer their labor.[52] In the case of parish churches the duty of providing the furnishings devolves upon the patron, those who derive income from the church, and finally the parishioners. The Code adds very wisely that in so far as the people of the diocese or of the parish are concerned, it is better to try to persuade them to donate rather than to force them to do so.[53] The same order of responsibility in the matter of providing the sacred furnishings holds in the case of other churches, *servatis servandis*.[54] From what has been said about the funds of the church, it is evident that ordinarily the sacred furnishings will be purchased by means of these funds. However, the Code in canon 1297 allows for the making of provision through other means. Thus, for example, special collections could be taken up for this purpose.[55] Or, as is the case in many parishes of the United States, the entire duty of the care, preservation, and supply of the sacred furnishings is left to the Altar Society.[56]

51 Coronata, *Inst. Iur Can.*, II, n. 760; Augustine, *A Commentary on the New Code of Canon Law* (2 ed., 8 vols., St. Louis: B. Herder Book Co., 1918-1924) (hereafter cited as *Commentary*), VI, 61.

52 S.C. Ep. et Reg., *Camerinen.*, 10 dec. 1841—*Fontes*, n. 1933.

53 Canon 1186, 1° and 2°.

54 Canon 1186, 3°.

55 Blat, *Commentarium Textus Codicis Iuris Canonici* [5 vols. in 6 (Vol. III, Pars altera, 1923), Romae, 1919-1927], III, Pars altera, n. 168.

56 Beste, *Introductio in Codicem* (ed. alt., Collegeville, Minn.: St. John's Abbey Press, 1944), p. 683.

CHAPTER V

OWNERSHIP OF THE SACRED FURNISHINGS OF DECEASED CLERICS

Historical Note

The outlawing of spoliage in the strict sense implied that a cleric had no right to dispose of the goods which he received as a result of his benefice. Canon 15 of the III General Council of the Lateran (1179) decreed that the cleric was bound to leave to his benefice the goods which he had acquired as a result of his tenure of it.

However, the idea that a cleric was under the *patriapotestas* of the bishop quite naturally gave birth to the idea that the cleric was a member of a new family of which the Holy Father is the *pater-familias.* Hence, from a juridical approach he was no longer considered to be a member of his blood family. As a result, the descent of his estate was determined, not from any considerations of blood, but in consequence of juridical enactments based on his juridical status, that is to say, legislation placed his juridical family rather than his natural family in the position of his heir. Consequently, at least from the fourteenth century onward the Holy See began to reserve to the Apostolic Camera the property of clerics who died intestate.[1]

St. Pius V (1566-1572) exempted the sacred furnishings of deceased clerics from the law of spoliage of the Apostolic Camera and decreed that these furnishings should escheat to the churches over which these clerics had presided.[2]

Pope Urban VIII (1623-1644),[3] and after him, Pope Benedict XIV (1740-1758),[4] issued legislation regarding the sacred furnish-

[1] Jerome D. Hannan, *The Canon Law of Wills* (The Catholic University of America Canon Law Studies, n. 86, Washington, D. C.: The Catholic University of America, 1934), nn. 267-268.

[2] Const. *Romani Pontificis,* 30 aug. 1567, n. 1—*Fontes,* n. 123.

[3] Const. *Aequum est,* 19 iul. 1642—*Fontes,* n. 225.

[4] Const, *Inter arduas,* 22 apr.—1749, §§-9—*Fontes,* n. 396.

ings of deceased Cardinals. This legislation included a brief history of the matter which is helpful in understanding the matter.

During their stay at Avignon (1305-1378) the Popes built a magnificent chapel as a part of their palace. After they returned to Rome they retained the custom of frequently performing in the Vatican Palace such solemn functions as were formerly celebrated in the basilicas. In these functions they were assisted by the Cardinals and the entire papal chapel. The Cardinals, too, held pontifical ceremonies which required more than ordinary sacred furnishings; these were purchased partly by the prelates themselves, partly by the papal treasurer. These furnishings were from time immemorial bequeathed to the papal chapel; hence there was established a precedent which appeared to be a juridical prescription.[5]

The final legislation regarding the sacred furnishings of all deceased clerics, Cardinals, residential bishops, and beneficed clerics, was formulated by Pope Pius IX (1846-1878).[6] It is this legislation that has become incorporated in the *Codex Iuris Canonici* practically in its entirety.[7]

Article I. The Sacred Furnishings of Deceased Cardinals Who Had Their Domicile in the City of Rome

The subjects of the law of papal seizure, as indicated in canon 1298, §1, are those Cardinals only who had their domicile in the City of Rome, even though they may have been suburbicarian bishops or abbots *nullius;* the latter are those Cardinals who, though they had obtained an abbacy *nullius,* still retained residence in the Curia.[8]

The sacred furnishings of the Cardinals which come within the scope of this canon comprise all the furnishings: mitres, copes, tunics, ornaments, vestments, chalices, patens, gold and silver vessels, utensils, and other things, especially those which have been consecrated or blessed;[9] sandals, gloves, linen amices, albs, cinc-

[5] Benedictus XIV, const. *Inter arduas,* §1.

[6] Litt. ap *Quum illud,* 1 iun. 1847—*Fontes,* n. 505.

[7] Canons 1298-1300.

[8] Pius IX, litt. ap. *Quum illud,* 1 iun. 1847, n. 1°—*Fontes,* n. 505.

[9] Urbanus VIII, const. *Aequum est,* §2.

tures, pyxes, holy water vessels and sprinklers, thuribles, oil stocks, cruets and basins, croziers, faldstools, palmatories, instruments of peace, and similar articles.[10]

The two phrases "utensils and other things" and "similar articles" appear to include every possible sacred furnishing. The Code, too, simply speaks of all sacred furnishings and all other things permanently devoted to divine worship. This category of furnishings seems to include also such articles as are serviceable for profane uses by their nature, but still are actually used for divine services and sacred functions permanently, and not only occasionally, for example, an ornate throne;[11] these appear to be what may be termed sacred furnishings in the broad sense.[12]

Exception is made in canon 1298, §1, only for the rings and the pectoral crosses, even though the latter contain sacred relics. As to this last item, the Cardinals are given more freedom than the bishops, whose pectoral crosses with the relics of the True Cross escheat to their cathedral churches.[13]

However, the pre-Code law had indicated other exceptions: for a Cardinal Deacon, one tunic; for a Cardinal Priest, one chasuble; for a Cardinal Bishop, one cope. Moreover, candalabra, pitchers and basins, even though they were of gold or silver, were also excepted from the general rule of the law.[14] Augustine argued that, inasmuch as these exceptions do not receive a specific mention in the present law, they are no longer in force.[15] However, as was noted above,[16] the present law is taken substantially from the Apostolic Letter *Quum illud,* which by its own statement is an interpretation of the Constitution *Aequum est;* the latter enumerates the exceptions just mentioned, and the former does not specifically set them aside as abrogated. Legally, then, it seems quite logical

[10] Pius IX, litt. ap. *Quum illud,* n. 3°.

[11] Vermeersch-Creusen, *Epitome,* II, n. 626.

[12] Cf. *supra,* pp. 17-18.

[13] Hannan, *op. cit.,* n. 319.

[14] Const. *Aequum est,* §2.

[15] *Commentary,* VI, 272.

[16] Cf. p. 28.

to conclude that, in virtue of canon 6, 2°, the exceptions are still in force.[17]

Furthermore, canon 1298, §1, states that all of the Cardinals' furnishings come within the scope of the law, regardless of their quality, and regardless of their source, that is, regardless of how the Cardinal obtained them, whether by purchase with personal or church funds, or whether by donation or gift.[18] Included also are those sacred furnishings which were used by them in their private chapels.[19]

Canon 1298, §1, prescribes the following regulations regarding the disposition of the sacred furnishings of these Cardinals upon their demise: a) if the Cardinal dies intestate, the law of papal spoliage takes effect, that is to say, all of the sacred furnishings enumerated above, except the specific exceptions made by the law, escheat to the papal sacristy. This would also be the case in the event that the instrument of bequest were invalid.[20]

b) If the Cardinal left a will or other instrument of bequest, the only possible beneficiaries of the Cardinal's generosity are any ecclesiastical persons, physical or moral, that is to say, a church, a public oratory, a pious place, or some ecclesiastical or religious person.[21]

It is immediately clear that these furnishings, even in virtue of a will, cannot be left to whomsoever the Cardinal chooses. His power of bequeathing is limited to the persons, physical or moral, enumerated in canon 1298, §1. These include priests, professed religious, religious communities, institutes of religious without vows, and ecclesiastical corporations duly established by ecclesiastical authority.[22] Private oratories cannot be made the recipients of the Cardinal's bequest; this includes the Cardinal's own private oratory.[23]

A problem of some moment could arise in the following case:

[17] Coronata, *Ins. Iur. Can.*, II, n. 880, fn. 7.
[18] Coronata, *op. cit.*, II, n. 880.
[19] Const. *Requum est*, §2.
[20] Coronata, *Inst. Iur. Can*, II, n. 880.
[21] Canon 1298, §1.
[22] Hannan, *The Canon Law of Wills*, n. 319.
[23] Const. *Inter arduas*, n. 7.

let it be supposed that one of the Cardinals were to give away some of these furnishings while he is still living. Would the donee be forced to give up his donation upon the demise of the Cardinal, that is to say, would he have to turn over these furnishings to the papal sacristy? Blat argues that the donee would have to yield his bequest;[24] however, there appears to be no basis for such an assumption in the present law.[25]

Canon 1298, §2, advises that it is most desirable for Cardinals, if they should wish to make use of the faculty, to donate at least some of the sacred furnishings to the churches held by them in title, in administration, or in commendam. Such a preference was also recommended by Popes Benedict XIV and Pius IX.[26] This is, of course, an admonition and not a precept.[27]

The reason given by some authors for the limitation with which canon 1298, §§1-2, qualifies the rightful transmission of a Cardinal's sacred furnishings is the forestalling of all irreverence that could result from the public sale of such furnishings.[28] This appears to be a specious argument in view of that fact that canons 1299-1300, which deal with the sacred furnishings of other clerics, do not place such a limitation upon these clerics in the making of their wills. There is no reason to presume that all danger of irreverence on the part of their heirs is any less likely to occur than on the part of the Cardinals' heirs. The chief reason for the limitation seems rather to be contained in history, that is to say, in the customary and traditional practices as reaching into the present.[29]

Article II: The Ownership of the Sacred Furnishings of Deceased Residential Bishops

The subjects of the law of canon 1299 are all residential bishops, whether they possess or whether they lack the dignity of the Car-

24 *Commentarium Textus Codicis Iuris Canonici,* III, n. 169.
25 Coronata, *Inst. Iur. Can.,* II, n. 880.
26 Const. *Inter arduas* and litt. ap. *Quum illud.*
27 Coronata, *Inst. Iur. Can.,* II, n. 880.
28 Coronata, *op. cit.,* II, n. 880.
29 Cf. *supra,* p. 27.

dinalate. Suburbicarian bishops are not subject to this law.[30] Abbots and prelates *nullius,* however, do come under the law.[31]

The sacred furnishings of the bishops as here contemplated in the law include the following: mitres, chasubles, copes, tunics, dalmatics, sandals, gloves, albs, cinctures, linen amices and the like; also, books of chant and music, missals, graduals, pontifical books, books of the *Canon of the Mass;* chalices, patens, pyxes, monstrances, thuribles, holy water vessels and sprinklers, cruets and basins, oil stocks, bells, palmatories, instruments of peace, archiepiscopal crosses, candalabra and crucifixes for use on the altar, croziers, faldstools; also other sacred articles, whether vestments, or ornaments, or vessels, even though their nature is not foreign to profane uses, provided, of course, that they are permanently, and not merely transitorily, dedicated to divine worship and sacred functions.[32] In a word, it appears that all of the sacred furnishings of bishops are included under the law.

All of these sacred furnishings, with the exceptions noted below, escheat to the cathedral church upon the demise of the bishop. The legislator has forseen that difficulties might arise when a bishop has ruled more than one diocese simultaneously, in view namely of the fact that the dioceses were united *in perpetuum,* or, at least for the lifetime of the incumbent, although each diocese still retained its own proper and distinct cathedral church. In such cases an equitable division is to be made according to the following regulations.

The sacred furnishings which are known to have been obtained with the funds of any particular diocese escheat to the cathedral church of that diocese. If it is impossible to establish with what funds the articles were purchased, two situations are possible: if the incumbency was simultaneous, and the income from all or the two dioceses constituted one *mensa episcopalis,* then the property is indivisible. If, on the contrary, the incumbency was successive, the property is considered to be divisible. The mere fact that the furnishings were not kept separate, although they had been pur-

30 Hannan, *The Canon Law of Wills,* n. 320.
31 Canon 215.
32 S. Pius V, const. *Romani Pontificis,* 30 aug. 1567, §1—*Fontes,* n. 123.

chased with various funds, does not constitute the property as indivisible; it would be necessary in such a case to consult the documents, invoices, and other available memoranda.[33] If the property is indivisible, that is to say, if the *mensa episcopalis* was administered as a single unit, the sacred furnishings of the deceased bishop are to be divided equally[34] among the cathedral churches over which he had ruled.

If, on the contrary, the property is divisible, that is to say, if the revenues from the various dioceses were distinct and separate, the sacred furnishings of the deceased bishop are to be divided among the cathedral churches over which he ruled in proportion to the amount of revenue he had received from each diocese and the length of time he presided over it.[35]

The ordinary rule as enacted in canon 1299 is that the sacred furnishings of deceased residential bishops escheat to their cathedral churches. The law, however, exempts two categories of furnishings from this rule. The first category connotes an absolute exception, namely, the bishops' rings and pectoral crosses are not subject to this law of seizure. It must be noted, however, that pectoral crosses which contain a relic of the True Cross accrue to the bishop's successor.[36]

[33] Hannan, *The Canon Law of Wills,* n. 321.

[34] *"Aequis partibus."*

[35] Hannan, (*The Canon Law of Wills,* p. 205, fn. 154) gives several examples of the *praxis curiae.*

Where a bishop had ruled one diocese eleven years, and another, two years, only the vestments were given to the cathedral church of the latter —S.C.C. in *Causa Suessana seu Catacen.,* 28 sept. 1709—*Fontes,* n. 3081; the same case, 25 jan., 1710—*Fontes,* n. 3084.

Where a bishop had been a few months in one diocese and seventeen years in another, even the vestments were awarded to the cathedral church of the latter because it was established that they had belonged to his predecessor in that see and had been lent to the decedent—S.C.C. *in Causa Trivicana seu Tricaricen.,* 8 iun. and 6 iul. 1726—*Fontes,* n. 3320.

Where an archbishop was but the administrator of another diocese, the latter was still entitled to its proportionate share of this property.—S.C.C. in *Trecen.,* 30 aug. 1845—*Fontes,* n. 4090.

[36] Canon 1288. Hannan, (*The Canon Law of Wills,* n. 320), states that even the suburbicarian bishops are bound to transmit to their successors the relics of the True Cross, as this canon demands.

The second category of sacred furnishings which do not escheat to the cathedral church of a deceased bishop is that regarding which there is legitimate proof that the furnishings were obtained with other than church funds and thereafter were not turned over to the proprietorship of the church. In other words, those sacred furnishings which through proof are acknowledged as having been the personal property of the bishop do not escheat to the cathedral church; they accrue to his heirs.[37]

The legislator also foresaw the difficulty which upon the demise of a bishop could arise in the matter of determining whether the sacred furnishings were personal property, i.e., obtained by the bishop with personal funds or as a personal donation, or whether they had been obtained with church revenues or as a donation to the church. To settle this difficulty, canon 1299, §3, orders that the bishop is obliged to construct an inventory of the sacred furnishings. This inventory must be drawn up in authentic form; it should note the value of the furnishing when it was acquired; it should clearly indicate whether the articles were purchased with the funds of the church, or with his own personal funds, whether they were gifts made to him personally or made to the church. This inventory is considered to be in authentic form if it is signed and sealed by the bishop.[38] Hannan notes that the III Plenary Council of Baltimore (1884) in its Decree N. 268 and N. 269 requires that the bishops of the United States construct a double inventory: in the one they are to list all the property belonging to the church; in the other, their personal property.[39]

The law accepts such an inventory as a positive proof in the point of determining the ownership of the sacred furnishings of a deceased bishop. In fact, Canon 1299, §3, states that in the event that there is no inventory it is presumed that all the sacred furnishings were purchased with church funds. Hence, there is a presumption of law in favor of the church.

However, if it can be proved, either by means of such an inventory, or through other means, that the sacred furnishings were pur-

[37] Coronata, *Inst. Iur. Can.*, II, n. 881.

[38] Coronata, *op. cit.*, II, n. 881.

[39] *The Canon Law of Wills*, n. 323.

chased with other than church funds, they would accrue to his heirs, even though these could not prove that the bishop had not given them to the church. The presumption which according to canon 1299, §3, militates in favor of the church does not extend to this situation; furthermore, canon 1299, §1, requires positive proof on the part of the church that the furnishings had been turned over to the proprietorship of the church.

Article III: The Ownership of the Sacred Furnishings of Other Deceased Clerics

1. The Sacred Furnishings of Beneficed Clerics

Canon 1300 specifies that the disposition of the sacred furnishings of any cleric who has obtained a secular or a religious benefice in any church is to be governed by the rules enacted in canon 1299 regarding the disposition of the sacred furnishings of deceased residential bishops. Hence, unless, the cleric has constructed an inventory, the presumption regarding the proprietorship of the sacred furnishings will favor the church, so that they will escheat to the church of the cleric's benefice. This presumption holds not only regarding the sacred furnishings used in the church itself, but also regarding those which were used in private chapels.[40] In like manner, even if at the time of his demise he no longer held a benefice, the latter would still have some claim against his sacred furnishings in the absence of proof to show that they were personal property.[41]

If the cleric held more than one benefice, then the rules applicable to the disposition of the sacred furnishings of a deceased residential bishop would hold. Thus, in case he holds benefices in which the union is of a co-ordinative[42] or a subordinative character[43] and the properties are distinguishable, the sacred furnishings will escheat to that benefice with whose funds they were purchased; if the properties are distinguishable, the sacred furnishings will be divided

[40] Coronata, *Inst. Iur. Can.*, II, n. 882.

[41] Benedictus XIV, const. *Ad honorandum*, 27 mart. 1752, §27—*Fontes*, n. 420.

[42] Canon 1419, 2°.

[43] Canon 1419, 3°.

equally. If the cleric holds benefices successively, and it cannot be determined what particular funds were employed for the purchase of the sacred furnishings, then these will be divided in proportion to the amount of revenue the cleric has received from each and according to the length of his tenure there.

2. The Sacred Furnishings of Other Deceased Clerics

Regarding the disposition of the sacred furnishings for clerics other than those mentioned in canons 1298-1300, the Code does not make any provisions. However, it appears logical that the rules of canon 1299 should apply to their furnishings also.[44] There are certainly clerics who never hold benefices but who exercise priestly functions in churches or oratories and who purchase sacred furnishings for such churches or oratories with funds donated by the faithful. The intention of the donors should not be frustrated; it appears quite normal to presume that they intend to provide sacred furnishings for use in the church and not merely for the convenience of the cleric.[45] However, the presumption of law in favor of the church as stated in canon 1299, §3, would not be applicable to the sacred furnishings of this category of clerics because of the patent lacuna in the law.[46]

The *raison d' ètre* of the law of canons 1299-1300 appears to lie in the fact that, although the revenues of a benefice accrue to the beneficiary, nonetheless such revenues carry with them an onus, e.g., canon 1473 imposes the obligation of expending the superfluous revenues (i.e., those that are not needed for the clerics *honesta sustentatio*) on the poor or for pious causes. In the case of the sacred furnishings, it seems the more proper thing to bequeath them to the church than to dispose of them freely.[47]

Article IV: The Formal Execution of the Foregoing Provisions Regarding the Sacred Furnishings of Deceased Clerics

In spite of the regulations enacted in canons 1298-1300, one can

[44] Coronata, *Inst. Iur. Can.*, II, n. 882; Augustine, *Commentary*, VI, 276.

[45] Coronata, *op. cit., loc. cit.*

[46] Coronata, *loc. cit.*

[47] Wernz-Vidal, *Ius Canonicum*, Tom. IV, vol. 1, n. 418.

readily visualize the difficulty which would be involved should one of these clerics die intestate with no indication as to the actual ownership of the property. The civil law in many countries, the United States included, may perhaps not take cognizance of the provisions of Canon Law. Hence the Code places upon Cardinals with a domicile in Rome, upon residential bishops, and upon beneficed clerics, the obligation of making a will or some other instrument which will be recognized as valid by the civil law in order that the provisions of canons 1298-1300 be carried out also in the civil courts.[48]

Furthermore, these clerics are, in good time, to appoint, also in a manner recognized by the civil law, a person of good repute, who upon their demise will take possession not only of their sacred furnishings but also of the books, documents, and all other property belonging to the church and found in their house, and turn them over to the proper authority.[49]

This agent is the equivalent of what is known as an executor. However, it appears to be the mind of the law that he is rather the representative of the church to assert the claims of the church against the estate of the decedent.[50]

In the United States, the necessity of making a will to guarantee a proper possession of the sacred furnishings is only a matter of added precaution. An authentic inventory or a formal statement made by the cleric is more important and would meet the requirements of the civil law.[51]

By varying such a statement somewhat he could make it a will. But a will has several disadvantages:

> First, it would be subject to all the restrictions which the secular law imposes on wills. . . . The second objection is that a will usually implies an assumption of ownership. Consequently, where there is no ownership, a will might be regarded as objectionable, when other legal means are adequate. The third reason is that the secular

---

[48] Canon 1301, §1.

[49] Canon 1301, §2.

[50] Hannan, *The Canon Law of Wills,* n. 333.

[51] Hannan, *op. cit.,* n. 325.

law does not favor subterfuges, and that would seem to be the character of a will made concerning property one does not own. The secular law regards itself as competent to protect the rights of owners and of claimants of property held by a decedent but not owned by him.[52]

---

[52] Hannan, *The Canon Law of Wills,* n. 327.

CHAPTER VI

PROVISION OF THE SACRED FURNISHINGS

The term "provision" as here used points to the use of the sacred furnishings as made available for others; that is to say, whom must or may a particular church permit to use its sacred furnishings. The law of the Code as expressed in canon 1303 divides the matter into two general considerations, namely the obligation to provide the sacred furnishings for the bishop and the obligation to provide them for other clerics.

Article I: For Use by the Bishop

The general law[1] obliges the cathedral church to permit the bishop to use its sacred furnishings gratuitously. It is quite apparent that the residential bishop or the bishop of the place is entitled to this gratuitous use of the sacred furnishings. Inasmuch as the Code does not make any distinction, it appears permissible to conclude that all bishops who happen to be attached to a diocese—coadjutors, auxiliaries, and apostolic administrators—are entitled to this gratuitous use.[2]

This gratuitous use of the sacred furnishings for the bishop extends to the use of all those sacred furnishings which are necessary for the proper performance of pontificial functions. Hence, the bishop is entitled not only to the use of those furnishings which he personally uses in such ceremonies, but also to the use of all such furnishings as may be needed by those assisting him in the performance of pontifical functions, as required by the laws of the liturgy.[3] Hence, for a Solemn Pontifical Mass to be celebrated from the throne the bishop has a claim for being provided with the following furnishings: amice, alb, cincture, stole, tunic, dalmatic, chasuble, mitres, gloves, pectoral cross, ring, crozier, *Missal, gremiale, bugia, Benedictional* (for the Pontifical blessing),

[1] Canon 1303, §1.

[2] Coronata, *Inst. Iur. Can.*, II, n. 884.

[3] Vermeersch, *Epitome,* II, n. 630; S.R.C., *Vercellen.,* 14 mart. 1643—*Fontes,* n. 5427.

Canon, book of the gospels, chalice, subdeacon's veil, book of the epistles and gospels, cruets of wine and water, pitcher with a basin and towel, bell, two candles, shoes and sandals, thurible and boat, processional cross, cope for the assistant priest; dalmatics, and amices for the assistant deacons; the ordinary vestments required for the deacon and subdeacon of the Mass; tunic, cincture, alb and amice for the subdeacon who is to carry the processional cross; two veils for the ministers who take care of the crozier and the mitres.[4]

Moreover, even though the bishop is not pontificating, that is to say, even when he says Mass privately, the law entitles him to the free use of the sacred furnishings of the cathedral church which he needs for this function.[5]

This gratuitous provision on the part of the cathedral church is due to the bishop not only when he pontificates or says Mass privately in the cathedral, but also when he holds these functions in other churches of the episcopal city or its suburbs. On such occasions it is still the obligation of the cathedral church to permit the bishop to use gratuitously all the sacred furnishings he needs.[6] It is of no moment how distant from the cathedral church is the church in which the bishop is holding the function, provided of course that the church be within the confines of the episcopal city or its suburbs.[7] However, it appears logical to expect that the expenses of transporting the sacred furnishings on such occasions should be defrayed by the church which enjoys the use thereof.[8]

Although the law appears to be quite generous in permitting the bishop to use the sacred furnishings of the cathedral church, it seems that it cannot be stated with certainty that the cathedral is obliged to provide these furnishings gratuitously when the

[4] Wapelhorst, *Compendium Sacrae Liturgiae iuxta Ritum Romanum,* ad novissima documenta recognovit et additiones passim locupletavit A. Bruegge (ed. 12a, Neo-Eboraci: Benziger Brothers, 1945). (Hereafter cited as *Compendium*), n. 159.

[5] Canon 1303, §1.

[6] Canon 1303, §1.

[7] Gasparri, *De SS. Eucharistia,* n. 670.

[8] G. Lardone, "Obbligo della cattedrale circa le suppelletti'li," *Perfice Munus* (Torino, 1926-) III (1928), 48.

bishop holds functions in his own chapel. Coronata alone among the post-Code authors brings up the point; he contends that a gratuitous providing of the furnishings is not due to the bishop in this case.[9] No legal arguments are presented for his opinion. However, inasmuch as the Code mentions only churches, it seems permissible to conclude that oratories could not be held favored in the same way as churches. Accordingly, the bishop's private chapel would seem to be excluded.

The Sacred Congregation of the Council, however, in its decrees *Urbevetana,* 19 ian., 9 febr., 1737,[10] expressly mentioned the right of the bishop to a gratuitous provision of the sacred furnishings of the cathedral church when he said Mass or held functions in his own chapel.[11] Gasparri, writing before the Code, held to the opinion that was thus expressed in the decisions of the Sacred Congregation of the Council.[12] He cited the decree *Terracinen. et Setina,* 14 dec. 1771:

> *Ad 3um: Affirmative, dummodo celebret in cathedrali vel in capella episcopali, et ad mentem. Mens est ut Episcopus provideat sacrarium ecclesiae juxta praescriptum in litteris apostolicis, et amplius.*[13]

The interesting note is that the bishop was expected to furnish the sacristy. If such was the case, it was incontrovertibly permissible for him gratuitously to use the sacred furnishings even when he celebrated any function in the episcopal chapel.

Furthermore, it can be argued that the phrase "even when he says Mass privately," can be taken to include the occasions when he does so in his chapel. This seems a legitimate interpretation in view of the pre-Code position and the decisions of the Congregation of the Council.

Modern authors conclude from canon 1303, §1, that any church in which the bishop holds functions is bound to provide its sacred furnishings to him gratuitously for use on such occasions.

9 *Inst. Iur. Can.,* II, n. 884.
10 *Fontes,* n. 3469.
11 *Fontes,* n. 3999.
12 *De SS. Eucharistia,* n. 670.
13 *Op. cit.,* n. 670.

However, such churches do not have the added obligation, as the cathedral has, of gratuitously providing the furnishings when functions are held in other near-by churches. Church A, for instance, does not have to provide any sacred furnishings gratuitously for the bishop when he holds a function in Church B.[14]

The basis for the law which required the cathedral church gratuitously to provide the sacred furnishings for episcopal functions held in other churches of the episcopal city or its suburbs apparently lies in the fact that generally it is only the cathedral church that has the sacred furnishings which are necessary for full pontifical ceremonies. The churches could not all be expected to purchase such an array of furnishings, for the simple reason that the furnishings would be so very rarely used, in most instances not even once a year. Hence, although the cathedral church could not by law be compelled to do so, one could equitably expect it to provide its furnishings gratuitously wheresoever in the diocese the bishop holds pontifical functions, at least with respect to those furnishings that are ordinarily lacking in parish churches.

Article II: For Use by Other Clerics

Although the Code itself does not specifically consider the matter of providing the sacred furnishings for use by clerics other than bishops, some conclusions regarding it can be deduced from canons 804 and 1303, §2-§4. Canon 804 specifies which extern[15] priests must or may be permitted to say Mass in a particular church; canon 1303, §2-§4, does not treat specifically with the supplying of the sacred furnishings, but rather specifies the circumstances which must prevail before a fee or a tax can be charged for their use. The consideration of these two canons will be the basis for determining the extent of the provision of the sacred furnishings which the law expects particular churches to make for clerics other than bishops.

It should be noted that for those priests who are in some way attached to a church, e.g., the parish assistants, the Code makes

[14] Coronata, *Inst. Iur. Can.*, II, n. 884; Wernz-Vidal, *Ius Canonicum,* Tom. IV, vol. 1, n. 421.

[15] This word is used to designate a cleric not attached to the church.

no regulations as to their right to say Mass in the church in which they are attached. In view of this connection, however, it is readily to be assumed that they not only have a right to say Mass in such a church, but also a duty to do so. Hence, they cannot be legally prohibited from saying Mass in such a church.[16]

For extern priests, canon 804 indicates specific rules to be followed regarding their admission to a church in order to say Mass. Under the following circumstances extern priests must be admitted to say Mass: a) a secular priest who has a valid letter of recommendation (commonly called celebret) from his ordinary; b) a religious priest who has such a letter from his superior; c) a priest of the Oriental rite who has such a letter from the Sacred Congregation for the Oriental Church. If any of these priests present valid celebrets, the law requires that they be admitted to the church to say Mass, unless it is known that meanwhile they have done something for which admission should be denied.[17]

If an extern priest when requesting admission to say Mass does not have a celebret, the rector of the church may permit him to say Mass if he knows that the priest is in good standing. Furthermore, even though the extern be unknown to the rector, the latter may permit him to say Mass once or twice, provided that he is wearing the ecclesiastical garb; that he receives no remuneration under any title from that church for the celebration of Mass, and that he records his name, his office, and the name of his diocese in a book to be specially kept for that purpose.[18]

The last paragraph of canon 804 specifies that the local ordinary has the right to make other special regulations regarding this matter. These regulations must not be contrary to the ones enacted in this canon, and they must be observed by all alike, even by exempt religious, except when there is question of admitting one of their own order to say Mass in their own church.

From these statements of the law it is clear that under certain conditions extern priests must or may be admitted to say Mass.

16 Cappello, *De Sacramentis,* I, n. 700. Vermeersch-Creusen, *Epitome,* I, n. 631.

17 Canon 804, §1.

18 Canon 804, §3.

Whether these externs, together with those who are in some way attached to the church, are to be served with a gratuitous provision of the sacred furnishings is a point not specifically covered by the law, and it constitutes a moot point among the authors. If a priest has a right or a duty to say Mass in a particular church, then it appears that he also has the right to use the sacred furnishings of that church which are necessary for the celebration of Mass. Further, the wording and tenor of canon 1303, §2-§4, seem to indicate that generally the needed furnishings should be supplied gratuitously.

This same canon deals with a tax or a fee which may be charged for the use of the sacred furnishings under certain conditions. Paragraph 2 states that the ordinary may permit a particular church to exact a moderate charge or tax for the providing of the sacred furnishings and other articles (e.g., altar breads, wine) necessary for the celebration of Mass from those priests who say Mass in the church for their own convenience, in the event that the church is indeed poor.[19]

From the wording of this canon it appears quite clear that ordinarily no charge should be made for the use of the sacred furnishings necessary for Mass. The particular church is not free to exact a tax for the providing of the sacred furnishings; this is a matter which is left to the judgment of the ordinary.

Canon 1303, §3, further specifies that by the ordinary in this case is meant only the bishop, not the vicar capitular, or the vicar general without a special mandate; only the bishop has the authority of determining the amount of the tax; in other words, only the bishop has the authority of determining what a moderate charge for the use of the sacred furnishings and other prerequisites for the celebration of Mass should amount to. In virtue of this statement of the Code, it seems logical to conclude that the law has in mind the ordinary of the place and not a religious ordinary. Vermeersch-Creusen argue to the contrary from the fact that

[19] Canon 1303, §2. Si qua ecclesia paupertate laboret, potest Ordinarius permittere ut a sacerdotibus qui in proprium commodum inibi celebrant, propter utensilia ceteraque ad Missae sacrificium necessaria, moderata stipes exigatur.

paragraph 2 of the same canon had not added to the word "ordinary" the qualifying phrase "of the place."[20]

According to canon 1303, §4, the Code wishes that this tax be determined for the whole diocese in the diocesan synod; lacking a synod, the tax may be determined by the ordinary after consulting the cathedral chapter. The legislator no doubt had in mind that the synodal law was to extend to the churches in which the ordinary decided the tax could be exacted in accord with canon 1303, §2.

The poverty of the church is the prime prerequisite for the exaction of this tax in consideration for the providing of the sacred furnishings. It might be admitted that the poverty could be only potential; for example, it is common knowledge that certain churches in Rome have hundreds of visiting clergy every year who wish to say Mass; if no tax were exacted, the treasury of such a church would suffer a considerable loss through its expenditures for altar breads, wine, candles, etc., not to mention the expenditures which would be entailed in the purchase of sacred furnishings as well as in their upkeep.

The disagreement among the authors regarding the gratuitous providing of the sacred furnishings for use by priests revolves around the two categories of priests mentioned above,[21] namely, those who are attached to a church in some way, and the externs.

With regard to those priests who are in some way attached to a church it is to be noted that there is an apparent lacuna in the law of the Code. Hence, those who argue against the gratuitous providing of the sacred furnishings for these priests base their argument on a pre-Code position, namely that of Gasparri, who held that a tax could be exacted from such priests.[22] He contended that the tax was payable whether the church was wealthy or poor. Admittedly these authors have no basis for their claim in

[20] *Epitome,* II, n. 631.

[21] Pp. 44-45.

[22] *De SS. Eucharistia,* n. 671; cf. Coronata, *Inst. Iur. Can.,* II, 884; Vermeersch-Creusen, *Epitome,* II, n. 631; Cocchi, *Commentarium in Codicem Iuris Canonici* (8 vols. in 5, Vol. V, ed. 4a, Taurinorum Augustae: Marietti, 1942) hereafter cited as *Commentarium,* V. n. 130.

the present law, as Vermeersch-Creusen point out: *"Regula generalis est, Codice non commemorata, ab iis qui titulo beneficii aut capellaniae celebrant in aliqua ecclesia et qui repelli non possunt seclusa peculiari conventione, percipi posse taxam utensilium."*[23]

On the opposite, and what appears to be the more tenable, side, Cappello[24] and Wernz-Vidal[25] contend that clerics attached to a church in some way have a right to a gratuitous provision of the sacred furnishings of that church. There is offered a very weighty reason, based on the law, namely, that the funds of the church, i.e., the *bona fabricae,* are precisely for the purpose of securing those things which are necessary for divine services; these certainly include the sacred furnishings.[26] But at the same time these authors admit that exceptions to the general rule are possible in virtue of custom, of contracts, and particular legislation.

A strange anomaly appears in the position of those who are opposed to mandatory granting of a gratuitous service to the attached clerics when they treat of the provision to be made for externs. In the latter case it is their position that, if a priest is permitted to say Mass in a church, that church should provide the sacred furnishings to him gratuitously.[27] Vermeersch-Creusen admit that only the actually involved expenses are to be paid.[28] These two authors appear to take a different position in their comment on canon 804 where they mention that the legislator, in permitting the various categories of extern priests to say Mass, seems to be fostering a *"fraternum commercium inter sacerdotes"* and make no mention of any tax except that stipulated by the bishop in favor of a poor church.[29]

It seems that the position of the protagonists for a gratuitous providing of the sacred furnishings to all priests alike is more in accord with the letter and the spirit of the law. As Cappello re-

[23] *Epitome, loc. cit.*
[24] *De Sacramentis,* I, n. 700.
[25] *Ius Canonicum,* Tom. IV, vol. 1, n. 421.
[26] Cf. *supra,* p. 23.
[27] Coronata, *Inst. Iur. Can., loc. cit.;* Cocchi, *Commentarium, loc. cit.*
[28] *Epitome, loc. cit.*
[29] *Epitome,* II, n. 76.

marks, where the custom of a gratuitous provision is now practiced, it should be continued, for such a custom is not only reasonable, but also laudable.[30]

Such a custom appears to exist in the United States, where, regularly at least, particular churches furnish visiting priests with all they need to say Mass free of charge.[31]

[30] *Op. cit.*, I, n. 700.

[31] Cf. H. Ayrinhac, *Administrative Legislation in the New Code of Canon Law* (London, New York, Toronto: Longmans, Green and Co., 1930), p. 173.

CHAPTER VII

BLESSING AND EXECRATION OF THE SACRED FURNISHINGS

ARTICLE I: NECESSITY FOR CONSECRATION OR BLESSING

The distinction previously made[1] between sacred furnishings in the strict sense and sacred furnishings in the broad sense made it clear that the word "sacred" derives not from the fact that the furnishings are necessarily consecrated or blessed, but rather from the fact that they are used habitually for divine services. Only sacred furnishings in the strict sense require a blessing or a consecration, whereby they obtain a certain spiritual character by which they are rendered fit for divine worship.[2]

The Code itself, in canons 1296, §1, and 1304, notes that certain of the sacred furnishings are to be consecrated or blessed in accord with the laws of the liturgy before they are used for their proper purpose in divine services. It should be noted that these same liturgical laws, as contained in the *Roman Missal,* the *Pontifical,* the *Ritual,* and the *Decrees of the Congregation of Rites,* nowhere recount an exhaustive list of the sacred furnishings which require a blessing or a consecration. Occasionally the rubrics of the *Missal* indicate that certain of the sacred furnishings are to be consecrated or blessed; the *Pontifical* and *Ritual* do not contain any such indications; the *Decrees of the Congregation of Rites* rarely mention anything about the need for blessing or consecration.

The authors appear to be agreed on an additional criterion for determining which of the sacred furnishings are to be consecrated or blessed, namely, the fact that the *Pontifical* or the *Ritual* contains the formula for a specific consecration or blessing for a particular furnishing. When such a formula exists, the authors conclude that the sacred furnishing in question should be consecrated

1 Cf. *supra,* pp. 14-16.

2 Thomas de Aquino, St., *Summa Theologiae* (5 vols., Ottawa: Studium Generale, O. PR., 1941-1945), Pars III, q. 83, art. 3, ad. 3.

or blessed before it is used in divine services.[3] This appears to be a valid criterion. It will be noted from canon 1304 that the sacred furnishings which require a blessing or a consecration can receive such a blessing or consecration only from those clerics who are indicated in the law as the proper ministers. Relative to the sacred furnishings, the formulas of consecrations and blessings which are contained in the *Pontifical* are reserved for use by the bishops; the formulas contained in the *Ritual* are listed under the headings: *"Benedictiones ab Episcopis vel ab aliis facultatem habentibus faciendae,"* and, in the Appendix, *"Benedictiones faciendae ab Ordinario vel ab eius delegato."* In like manner, whenever the *Missal* indicates that a furnishing is to be consecrated or blessed, it notes that it is to be done by the bishop or his delegate. Hence it seems quite reasonable to conclude that, whenever a specific formula for the consecration or the blessing of a furnishing is found in one of the liturgical books, the furnishing in question should be consecrated or blessed accordingly.

With these criteria in mind, one may proceed to the consideration of which of the sacred furnishings require a consecration or a blessing. The chalice and paten are the only sacred furnishings which are to be consecrated. The *Missal* notes that these are to be consecrated by the bishop.[4] The *Pontifical* contains the specific formula for the consecration of the chalice and the paten.[5] It is to be noted that the actual formula of consecration must be employed. The one-time apparently prevalent opinion that the use of these vessels for the celebration of Mass gave them an automatic consecration is untenable. This opinion was based on the response of the S.R.C., *Fulden.*, 22 sept. 1703, *ad* 3, which, however, does not appear in the *Decreta Authentica* of this Congregation.[6]

There is general agreement among the authors that the following

[3] Vermeersch-Creusen, *Epitome,* II, n. 632; Wernz-Vidal, *Ius Canonicum,* Tom. IV, vol. I, n. 419; Gasparri, *De SS. Eucharistia,* n. 710.

[4] Tit. *Ritus servandus in celebratione missae,* Cap. I, *De praeparatione sacerdotis celebraturi,* n. 1.

[5] Tit. *De patenae et calicis consecratione.*

[6] Cf. Cappello, *De Sacramentis,* I, p. 706, fn. (9); Còronata, *Inst. Iur. Can.,* II, n. 885. S.R.C., *Sancti Hippolyti,* 31 aug. 1867, ad VII—*Decr. Auth.,* n. 3162.

sacred furnishings must be blessed in accord with the rubrics of the Missal:[7] the altar cloths;[8] the corporal and pall;[9] the sacerdotal vestments which are enumerated as the amice, the alb, the cincture, the maniple, the stole, and the chasuble.[10]

There appears to be an opinion, noted by most of the authors, that the cincture does not require a blessing; the common opinion, however, is that the cincture is to be blessed.[11] Moreover, the tabernacle is to be blessed.[12]

It appears that inasmuch as the *Missal* does not mention any other sacred furnishings which require a blessing or a consecration, the authors in like manner, with the exception of Gasparri,[13] decline to say that any of the other sacred furnishings require such a blessing. Augustine notes that the monstrance, pyx, dalmatics, cope, and surplice may be blessed.[14] Vermeersch-Creusen add that the shoes and sandals are to be blessed, and likewise the pyx and the lunula of the monstrance; that the monstrance, cope, surplice, and purificator may be blessed; and that the humeral veil and the *gremiale* may be, but ordinarily are not blessed.[15] Coronata says that the pyx or the ciborium, the monstrance together with its lunula, the cope, dalmatics, tunics, and surplice may be blessed; that the humeral veil, chalice veil, burse, and purificator are not ordinarily, although they may be, blessed.[16]

7 Augustine, *Commentary,* VI, 268; Coronata, *op. cit.,* II, n. 885; Vermeersch-Creusen, *op. cit.,* II, n. 632; Cappello, *op. cit.,* I, nn. 749-759; Gasparri, *op. cit.,* n. 710.

8 *Missale Romanum,* Tit. *Rubricae generales,* Cap. XX, *De praeparatione altaris, et ornamentorum eius;* Tit. *De defectibus in celebratione missarum occurrentibus,* Cap. X, *De defectibus in ministerio ipso occurrentibus,* n. 1.

9 *Ibid.,* Tit. *Ritus servandus in celebratione missae,* Cap. I, n. 1; Tit. *De*

10 *Ibid.,* Tit. *Ritus servandus in celebratione missae,* Cap. I, n. 2-3.

defectibus in celebratione missae occurrentibus, Cap. X, n. 1.

11 Augustine, *op. cit. loc. cit.;* Coronata, *op. cit., loc. cit.;* Vermeersch-Creusen, *op. cit., loc. cit.;* Cappello, *op. cit.,* I, n. 758; Gasparri, *op. cit.,* n. 710.

12 S.R.C., *Romana,* 20 iun 1899, ad IV—*Decr. Auth.* n. 4035.

13 *Op. cit., loc. cit.*

14 *Commentary,* VI, 268.

15 *Epitome,* II, n. 632.

16 *Inst. Iur. Can.,* II, n. 885.

If, however, the general principle to be followed as above enunciated, namely, that those sacred furnishings are to be blessed for which a ritual of blessing is found in the liturgical books, then the following sacred furnishings require a blessing: the shoes, sandals, amice, alb, cincture, stole, maniple, tunic, dalmatic, and chasuble;[17] the altar cloths;[18] the corporal and pall;[19] the pyx or ciborium;[20] the pectoral cross; [21] the monstrance.[22]

The more common sacred furnishings which receive no mention in the liturgical books, that is, in so far as the necessity for a blessing is concerned, are: the burse, chalice veil, humeral veil, cope, purificator, *Missal,* altar cards, candlesticks, crucifix, frontals, cruets, thuribles, surplices. Gasparri noted that in Rome the cope is usually blessed, although this is not obligatory.[23] It appears that the altar cross and the processional cross may, but do not have to be blessed.[24]

It may be noted here that the corporal and the pall do not have to be blessed together, although the *Missal* indicates that a simultaneous blessing of them is the proper procedure.[25] The same procedure is intimated in the title and the formula of this blessing as

[17] *Pontificale Romanum,* Summorum Pontificum iussu editum, a Benedicto XIV et Leone XIII Pont. Max. recognitum et castigatum (Ratisbonae, 1908), *Benedictio specialis cuiuslibet indumenti; De benedictione sacerdotalium indumentorum in genere; Rituale Romanum,* Tit. VIII, c. 20, *Benedictio sacerdotalium indumentorum.*

[18] *Pontificale Romanum, De benedictione mapparum seu linteaminum sacri altaris; Rituale Romanum,* Tit. VIII, c. 21, *Benedictio mapporum seu tobalearum altaris.*

[19] *Pontificale Romanum, De benedictione corporalium; Rituale Romanum,* Tit. VIII, c. 22, *Benedictio pallae et corporalis.*

[20] *Pontificale Romanum, De benedictione tabernaculi sive vasculi pro sacrosancta Eucharistia conservanda; Rituale Romanum,* Tit. VIII, c. 23, *Benedictio tabernaculi seu vasculi pro sacrosancta Eucharistia conservanda.*

[21] *Pontificale Romanum, De benedictione crucis pectoralis.*

[22] *Rituale Romanum,* Appendix, Tit. *Benedictiones reservatae,* I, *Benedictione ab ordinario vel ab eius delegato,* n. 3, *Benedictio tabernaculi seu ostensorii pro sanctissimo Sacramento fidelium venerationi exponendo.*

[23] *Op. cit.* n. 710.

[24] S.R.C., *Urbis,* 12 iul. 1704—*Decr. Auth.,* n. 3697.

[25] Tit. *Ritus servandus in celebratione missae,* C. I, n. 1.

found in the *Ritual,* namely, the *Benedictio pallae et corporalis.*[26] The S.R.C., however, ruled that a separate blessing was permissible. It is also permissible to bless one pall and several corporals simultaneously, or one corporal and several palls simultaneously. In such cases the formula should be adapted to the particular situation.[27]

In conclusion, it appears that only the following sacred furnishings require the consecration or blessing as prescribed by the laws of the liturgy as noted in canons 1296, §1, and 1304: the chalice, paten, amice, alb, cincture, shoes, sandals, pectoral cross, maniple, stole, chasuble, pyx, ciborium, monstrance, altar cloths, corporal, pall, and tabernacle. It appears that the other sacred furnishings could be given a blessing, although such a blessing is not required by the law either of the Code or of the liturgy.

Article II: The Minister of the Blessing or Consecration of the Sacred Furnishings

Canon 1304 treats specifically about the minister of the blessing of the sacred furnishings, and not about the minister of the consecration thereof. Consecration in the strict sense, that is the unction with the Holy Oils, is reserved by law to consecrated Bishops alone, unless this faculty is given to a lower cleric either by the law itself or by apostolic indult.[28]

The law gives the faculty of consecrating sacred furnishings to the following persons: cardinals, even though they are not bishops;[29] vicars and prefects apostolic, even though they lack the episcopal character;[30] their temporary successors;[31] abbots and prelates nullius, although not consecrated as bishops.[32]

When any other cleric obtains the faculty of blessing the sacred furnishings, it is understood that such a faculty does not imply that

[26] Tit. VII, c. 22.
[27] S.R.C. *Briocen.,* 4 sept. 1880, ad III—*Decr. Auth.,* n. 3524.
[28] Canon 1147, §1.
[29] Canon 239, §1, 20.
[30] Canon 294, §2.
[31] Canon 310, §2.
[32] Canon 323, §2.

the cleric thereby becomes empowered also to consecrate the furnishings.[33]

Canon 1304 lists the persons who have the faculty to bless such sacred furnishings as require a blessing in accord with the laws of the liturgy before they are to be used for their proper purpose. These persons are:

1. All cardinals and bishops;
2. Local ordinaries who lack the episcopal character, for the churches and oratories within their territories;
3. Pastors, for the churches and oratories situated within the territories of their parishes; rectors of churches, for their churches;
4. Priests delegated by the local ordinary, within the limits of their delegation and of the jurisdiction of the delegator;
5. Religious superiors, and priests of the same religious institute when delegated by such superiors, for their own proper churches and oratories, and for the churches of nuns subject to these superiors.

The basis for this law is intimated in the phrase "in accord with the laws of liturgy." The latter always indicate that the minister of these blessings is the bishop or one delegated by him.[34] These blessings are enumerated in the *Pontifical,* and in the *Ritual* under those sections which contain blessings reserved to the bishop or to others having the faculty.[35] The Code merely points out who those clerics are in addition to bishops who have the faculty of blessing the sacred furnishings which according to the laws of the liturgy require an episcopal blessing.

This requirement of a special faculty to bless the sacred furnishings, as granted either by the law or in consequence of an act of delegation, simply touches the licitness of the act of blessing. A blessing of this kind, even though performed by a priest who lacks this faculty, would nonetheless be valid, though of course illicit. An exception would obtain only if the Holy See or the Code spe-

[33] S.R.C., *Cameracen.,* 11 mart. 1632—*Decr. Auth.,* n. 587; Augustine, *Commentary,* VI, 284; Coronata, *Inst. Iur. Can.,* II, n. 885.

[34] *Missale Romanum,* Tit. *Rubricae generales,* C. XX; Tit. *Ritus servandus in celebratione Missae,* C. I, n. 1.

[35] Cf. *supra,* p. 52.

cifically and expressly mentioned the need of the faculty as a condition for the validity of the blessing.[36] But regarding the blessings of the sacred furnishings no such specification seems anywhere extant. Deacons and lectors, on the contrary, would act not only illicitly but also invalidly if they attempted to bless the sacred furnishings.[37]

It is to be noted that any cleric who is not a consecrated bishop should use the formulas found in the *Ritual,* and not the ones found in the *Pontifical* for the blessing of the sacred furnishings. The negative import of this rule is to be followed even when the formula for the specific blessing which is being performed is lacking in the *Ritual;* for example, for the blessing of a stole, the formula which carries the title *Benedictio sacerdotalium indumentorum*[38] should be used.[39] However, if a priest were perchance to use the pontifical formula, the blessing would be valid.[40]

Except with reference to cardinals and consecrated bishops, the faculty of blessing the sacred furnishings is limited; it extends only to those furnishings which are to be used in a particular territory, oratory, or church. Thus, a non-episcopal local ordinary can personally or through others as his delegates bless only those sacred furnishings which are to be used in the churches or oratories of his diocese. The pastor can bless only those sacred furnishings which are for use in the churches or oratories of his parish. Priests delegated by the local ordinary can bless only the furnishings that are specified in the delegation itself, for the churches specified, and not outside the jurisdiction of the ordinary. The religious superior can bless or delegate another with the rightful power of blessing only such sacred furnishings as are to be used in the churches and oratories of his religious institute or in the churches of nuns subject to him. This faculty of blessing cannot be extended even to the sacred furnishings which are going to be given to poor churches.[41]

[36] Canon 1147, §3.

[37] Canon 1147, §4.

[38] *Rituale Romanum,* Tit. VII, c. 20.

[39] S.R.C., *Blesen.,* 16 mart. 1876—*Decr. Auth.,* n. 3392; *Imolen.,* 2 dec. 1881, *Decr. Auth.,* n. 3533.

[40] Coronata, *Inst. Iur. Can.,* II, 885.

[41] S.R.C., *Mechlinien.,* 31 aug. 1867, ad XI—*Decr. Auth.,* n. 3157.

However, once a sacred furnishing is blessed or consecrated, there is no need to re-consecrate or re-bless it when it is transferred to another church.[42]

The churches of nuns, as mentioned in canon 1304, §5, are those which in some way come under the jurisdiction of a religious superior, or are actually subject to him. Such are, for certain, the churches of the convents of those nuns which are subject to a regular superior, but the churches of tertiaries are not included unless they enjoy special privileges. Chaplains of the oratories of nuns or sisters do not enjoy the faculty of blessing the sacred furnishings to be used therein. It seems that such chaplains cannot be assimilated to rectors of churches for the purpose of blessing furnishings. Coronata, however, is of the opinion that these chaplains can be assimilated to rectors of churches when the nuns are subject to the local ordinary.[43]

A problem discussed by the authors is whether the pastor, granted that by the Code he has the faculty to bless the sacred furnishings,[44] can in view of this fact delegate the faculty which he seems to possess as an ordinary power attached to his office. Coronata,[45] Vermeersch-Creusen,[46] Wernz-Vidal[47] and Cicognani[48] argue that the pastor is not thereby authorized to delegate this faculty. This negative attitude derives from three lines of argumentation. Coronata and Wernz-Vidal state that, even though it may be an ordinary power that by the Code is attached to the office of the pastor, nonetheless an implicit restriction is placed on the delegation thereon, since the very wording of canon 1304 precludes all notion of a possible delegation. These authors regard canon 1304 as recounting an all-inclusive list of those who can actually bless the sacred furnishings or delegate others to do so.

Cicognani, by a very similar process of reasoning, deduces that

42 Vermeersch-Creusen, *Epitome,* II, n. 633.

43 *Inst. Iur. Can.,* II, n. 885; cf. Augustine, *Commentary,* VI, 284.

44 Canon 1304, §3.

45 *Op. cit.,* II, n. 885.

46 *Op. cit.,* II, 663.

47 *Ius Canonicum,* Tom. IV, vol. 1, n. 419.

48 "De facultate benedicendi sacram supellectilem ex can. 1304, *Apollinaris* (Romae, 1928—) I, 65-66.

in this case the Code is not granting ordinary power attached to the office of the pastor, but rather that the faculty is given *"ad instar privilegii personalis"*; hence it is not to be delegated.

Vermeersch-Creusen, following what appears to be a more valid line of reasoning, think that inasmuch as it is a question of a power of blessing, the matter comes not under the category of the power of jurisdiction, but rather under the category of the power of orders. As such it would come under the scope of canon 210, which forbids the delegation of the power of orders unless such delegation is expressly permitted by the law itself or in virtue of an indult.

Cappello, who appears to be alone on this score, argues to the contrary, namely that the pastor and even the rector of a church can delegate this power of blessing the sacred furnishings. He contends that in this instance the Code in giving ordinary power and that, inasmuch as the law placed no restrictions on the delegation thereof,[49] the pastor and the rector may delegate it. Furthermore, the power in question is one of jurisdiction and not one of orders.[50] He argues further that the power of orders which derives from ecclesiastical law is not a power that is specifically distinct from the power of jurisdiction; rather, it proceeds from the power of jurisdiction and should be reduced to it as a part to the whole, or the species to the genus.[51] Hence, Cappello's argument contends that the Code is here granting the pastor ordinary power of jurisdiction, and that, if such be the case, that power can be committed to others by way of delegation.

Most of the authors, on the contrary, consider that a blessing postulates not indeed the power of jurisdiction but in reality the power of orders.[52] Furthermore, it should be noted that the Code itself in canon 210 makes no distinction between the power of orders deriving from the divine law and the power of orders deriving from the ecclesiastical law, as Cappello does, but simply mentions the power of orders. Furthermore, the very position in the Code

49 Canon 199, §1.

50 *De Sacramentis,* I, n. 89.

51 *Op. cit.,* I, n. 88.

52 Wernz-Vidal, *Ius Canonicum,* Tom. IV, vol. 1, n. 48; Vermeersch-Creusen, *Epitome,* I, n. 323; Coronata, *Institutiones Iuris Canonici, De Sacramentis* (3 vols., Romae: Marietti, 1943-1946), III, n. 727.

of the Title on Sacred Furnishings, namely in the section *De Cultu Divino,* appears to imply that the power of orders and not that of jurisdiction is to be understood. Hence it appears that Cappello's argument lacks cogency, and that pastors and rectors of churches cannot delegate this power for the reason given by Vermeersch-Creusen, namely, that the question turns on the power of orders and that the law has not made any specfic provision for its delegation in this case.

ARTICLE III: EXECRATION OR LOSS OF CONSECRATION OR BLESSING

Canon 1305, §1, states that the sacred furnishings lose their blessing or consecration in one of three ways: 1) if they undergo such damage or change that they lose their original form and are no longer fit and suitable for their purpose; 2) if they are used for unbecoming purposes, and 3) if they are exposed for public sale.

The loss of a blessing or a consecration as resulting through damage or change of the article or the furnishing was acknowledged before the advent of the present legislation in the Code.[53] The loss effected in consequence of the use of the furnishing for an unbecoming purpose or as the result of its being exposed for public sale points to a new law in the Code.[54]

Examples of the loss of a blessing or a consecration as caused through damage or through a change in form that renders the furnishing unfit for its purpose are: a complete separation of the sleeves from the alb;[55] the existence of a hole in the bottom of the cup of the chalice; a shortening of the cincture to the extent that it can no longer gird the priest;[56] the separation of the cup of the chalice from the stem because of a break (not, however, the act of unscrewing or unbolting the cup, for the chalice would not thus be subjected to any damage); the use of the linen of an alb for the making of corporals, palls, or amices (all of the latter would re-

[53] Wernz, *Ius Decretalium,* III, n. 504.
[54] Woywod, *A Practical Commentary,* II, n. 1324.
[55] Coronata, *Inst. Iur. Can.,* II, n. 886.
[56] Vermeersch-Creusen, *Epitome,* II, n. 634.

quire a new blessing). The same would be true if, for example, a chasuble were made from a cope.

Whether the damage or the change be deliberate or accidental, or whether it be occasioned in good or in bad faith, is irrelevant. It likewise is not of any moment whether the damage or the change be momentary in duration or protracted for some time. If the damage or the change is such that the furnishing loses its original form, it loses its blessing or consecration and must be re-blessed or reconsecrated before it is used again.

From the repairing of the sacred furnishing there does not result any execration, and hence there is no need for a new blessing or consecration, provided that the new part is not larger than the old; this holds true even though through successive repairs practically the entire furnishing eventually becomes replaced.[57]

While a deliberate execration effected in this manner could be considered reprehensible, it would be legitimate for a just cause, for example, for the converting of sacred furnishings, particularly such as are worn out or outmoded, to non-sordid profane uses.[58]

The mere profane use of a sacred furnishing, although illicit,[59] would not however entail execration. The purpose that is served must be something unbecoming or sordid. The classic example of such an unbecoming use is the use of the chalice as a drinking cup by heretics.[60] Other examples of unbecoming uses are not recounted by the authors; however, Augustine[61] and Coronata[62] state that there is no doubt that any use which is seriously sinful is unbecoming and therefore entails execration. The mere profane use of a sacred furnishing by a heretic does not cause a loss of blessing or consecration.[63]

Regarding the third way of execrating the sacred furnishings,

[57] Coronata, *op. cit., loc. cit.*

[58] Vermeersch-Creusen, *Epitome,* II, n. 634.

[59] Cf. *supra,* pp. 15-17.

[60] Coronata, *Inst. Iur. Can.,* II, n. 886, who cites Gasparri, *De SS. Eucharistia,* n. 752, who in turn cites a decree of the Holy Office of the year 1674.

[61] *A Commentary,* VI, 286.

[62] *Op. cit., loc. cit.*

[63] Coronata, *Inst. Iur. Can.,* II, n. 886.

namely by exposing or putting them up for public sale, it should be noted that it is not the sale itself which brings on execration, but the exposition or putting up for sale. Thus if a sacred furnishing were placed in an auction sale,[64] or if an advertisement were put in the paper among the want ads to indicate that a sacred furnishing is for sale, execration would be incurred. If, on the contrary, the sale is private, for example, one priest sells another priest a chalice, or one church sells another church a set of vestments, then there would not be any execration.

Special Note: Replating the Chalice and Paten

A new note is injected into the law of the Code regarding the replating of chalices and patens. Formerly, in accord with the ruling of the S.R.C., it was considered necessary to re-consecrate replated chalices and patens.[65] The present discipline in this matter, as indicated in the law of the Code in canon 1305, §2, is that chalices and patens do not lose their consecration because of replating. Formerly it seems to have been the custom in some places to make the chalice unfit for use for the purpose of execrating it before it was turned over to a commercial firm for re-plating. The S.R.C. condemns and forbids such a practice as an abuse.[66]

Canon 1305, §2, further specifies that whenever the plating of the chalice and the paten is worn off, there is a serious obligation to have it renewed. When there is need for such re-plating, the priest should obtain permission from the bishop to turn the vessels over to a firm for repairs.[67] In order to facilitate this matter, bishops usually designate certain firms to do the necessary replating and repairs on chalices and patens. When this procedure is followed, the priest need not obtain any further permission from the bishop.[68]

[64] Coronata, *Inst. Iur. Can.*, II, n. 886.

[65] S.C.R., *Leodien.*, 14 iun 1845—*Decr. Auth.*, n. 2889; Strigonien., 9 maii 1857—*Decr. Auth.*, n. 3042. Cf. also Gasparri, *De SS. Eucharistia*, n. 752.

[66] S.R.C., *Dubiorum*, 23 apr. 1822—*Decr. Auth.*, n. 2620.

[67] Woywod, *A Practical Commentary*, II, n. 1324.

[68] S.R.C., *Suffragium ad decretum* n. 2620—*Decr. Auth.*, IV, 223.

CHAPTER VIII

HANDLING AND WASHING OF THE SACRED FURNISHINGS

Article I: Handling of the Sacred Furnishings

The discipline regarding the handling of the sacred furnishings has undergone considerable relaxation from the time of the *Decree* of Gratian to its present status in the Code. The law of the *Corpus Iuris* was most strict in its insistence that the sacred vessels and vestments were to be handled only by clerics in major orders.[1]

Writing before the Code, Wernz (1842-1914) noted that in his time the ancient rigor had been relaxed to the extent that lay brothers, sisters, and even laymen acting as sacristans were allowed to handle the sacred vessels.[2] Gasparri, also a pre-Code author, noted the same relaxation in the Church's discipline. He noted that the current custom permitted all clerics, even those in minor orders, as well as lay-brother sacristans and sister sacristans, to handle the chalice and paten, corporals, palls, and purificators. These same furnishings could be handled by lay persons who were sacristans. The very fact that they were sacristans gave them a legitimate reason or cause for handling these furnishings. Furthermore, even if others, that is non-sacristans, handled them without irreverence they committed at most only a venial sin and most probably no sin at all.[3]

The law of the Code synthesizes and gives expression to this immediate pre-Code position. It states that care must be taken that the chalice and paten, and, before they have been laundered, the corporals, palls, and purificators, when they have been used in the sacrifice of the Mass, should not be touched except by clerics, or by those who have the custody of the sacred furnishings.[4]

[1] Cf. *supra*, p. 12.

[2] *Ius Decretalium*, III, n. 503.

[3] *De SS. Eucharistia*, II, n. 757.

[4] Canon 1306, §1.

The law seems to be very clear. The prohibition applies to the chalice and paten which have been consecrated and used in the Mass; it would not apply to these sacred vessels if they had not been consecrated and had not been used at Mass; neither would it apply to such vessels after they had been execrated.[5] Inasmuch as canon 1306, §1, specifically mentions only the chalice and paten among the sacred vessels, it seems that the same prohibition does not extend to other sacred vessels such as the pyx, the ciborium, and the monstrance.[6] Regarding the monstrance, however, the S.R.C. has ruled that the directions relative to the handling of the sacred vessels by the laity be observed. This seems to imply that at least the monstrance should be included among the vessels the touching of which is in canon 1306, §1, prohibited to the laity.[7]

Only three sacred linens, the adjuncts of the chalice, namely, the corporals, the palls, and the purificators, are listed under the prohibition. Hence altar cloths could not be included; however, it would be reasonable and in accord with the spirit of the law that the latter should be handled only by clerics or by sacristans under certain circumstances, for example, in the event that the Sacred Species had come into direct contact with them. It is only the unlaundered corporals, palls, and purificators that come under the prohibition; after these have been laundered, they may be handled by anyone.

It is clear that the present law, contrary to the law of the *Corpus Iuris Canonici,* allows all clerics, therefore all who have received tonsure, to handle the sacred vessels and linens in question. It should be noted, however, that the law here has reference to the handling of these furnishings outside the time of liturgical functions.

The other category of persons who are permitted by the law to handle these vessels and linens are those who have custody of them. This indicates that any person, religious or lay, who is the sacristan is allowed to handle these furnishings. This is only reasonable; it would be practically impossible for the sacristan to perform the duties of this office properly if he were prohibited

[5] Gasparri, *De SS. Eucharistia,* n. 757.

[6] Augustine, *A Commentary,* VI, 288; Coronata, *Inst. Iur. Can.,* II, n. 887.

[7] S.R.C., *Westmonasterien.,* 27 maii 1911, ad 6—*Decr. Auth.,* n. 4268.

from handling these furnishings. Hence, one may conclude that the law permits sister sacristans, lay-brother sacristans, and lay sacristans of either sex to handle the chalice, paten, and unlaundered used corporals, palls, and purificators.

Augustine, arguing from the wording of canon 1306, §2, represented the opinion that the phrase "those who have custody of them" presumes that such persons are to be clerics.[8] He is alone in this position, and it appears to be scarcely tenable. As Vermeersch-Creusen note,[9] the wording of canon 1306, §1, would be entirely unintelligible if others than clerics were excluded; the phrase reads: *"a clericis vel ab iis qui eorum custodiam habent."* The *vel* here used makes the phrase disjunctive, thereby adding another category of persons who are permitted to handle the sacred furnishings, namely, non-clerics who are sacristans.

It seems likewise to be entirely consonant with the law to admit that other persons, even though they are not sacristans, provided they have a reasonable cause for doing so, should apart from all fault be permitted to touch or handle these vessels and linens. Such a cause, for example, certainly arises when the chalice and paten must be sent to a firm for re-plating.[10] Further, it may even be said that the phrase "those who have custody of them" is broad enough to include the nature of a merely temporary custody or care, exercised for example on such occasions when the members of the Altar Society are cleaning in the sacristy, or when during a liturgical function the readying of one of these furnishings has been overlooked and it needs to be brought to the celebrant, or into the sanctuary.

However, it seems to be wholly in accord with the reverence due to sacred things that, whenever it becomes necessary for a non-sacristan to handle these vessels or linens, he do so with the aid of a clean cloth. Such a procedure seems particularly applicable in handling of the ciborium or the pyx.

Article II: Washing of the Sacred Linens

The relaxation in the rigor of the ancient discipline regarding

[8] *A Commentary,* VI, 288.
[9] *Epitome,* II, 887.
[10] Vermeersch-Creusen, *Epitome,* II, n. 635.

the handling of the chalice and the paten, as well as of the soiled corporals, pall and purificators, is not nearly so evident in regard to the washing of these sacred linens. The law of the *Corpus Iuris Canonici* required an elaborate ceremony performed only by clerics who at least were deacons.[11] The law of the Code still restricts the washing of purificators to clerics in major orders; however, there is no particular place or ceremony assigned for this operation. Canon 1306, §2, states that corporals, palls, and purificators, if they have been used in the sacrifice of the Mass shall not be turned over to lay persons or religious for laundering before these linens have been washed by a cleric in major orders; the water used for this first washing is to be poured into the sacrarium, or, if there is no sacrarium, into the fire.

These linens are to be washed in three distinct waters.[12] The Code refers only to the first washing. This is to be done by a cleric in major orders, that is say, by a priest, a deacon, or a subdeacon. The bishop is not allowed to authorize nuns, sisters, or lay brothers to do this first washing.[13] Such authorization could come only in virtue of an apostolic indult. Hence, under normal circumstances in the United States the duty of washing the sacred linens devolves upon the priests of the parish. It is quite the proper procedure, too, that a cleric in major orders wash the altar cloths in the event that the Precious Blood should somehow have been spilled thereon.

Although Coronata, apparently having in mind a major cleric, notes that a cleric performs all the three washings,[14] such a procedure hardly seems necessary. The latter part of canon 1306, §2, mentions only the water of the first washing.[15] It seems to be quite sufficient that a major cleric do only the first washing; thereupon these linens may be turned over to other persons, lay or religious, for the second and third washings and final laundering.[16]

The water which was used for this first washing is to be dis-

[11] Cf. supra, pp. 12-13.

[12] L. O'Connell, *The Book of Ceremonies* (Milwaukee: Bruce, 1943), p. 19.

[13] S.R.C., *Molinen.*, 12 sept. 1857, ad XXVI—*Decr. Auth.*, n. 3059.

[14] *Inst. Iur. Can.*, II, n. 887.

[15] "Aqua . . . primae lotionis . . ."

[16] L. O'Connell, *The Book of Ceremonies*, p. 19.

posed of in such a way as to avoid all danger of exposing it to irreverence. It is to be poured into the sacrarium; if there is no sacrarium, it is to be poured into a fire. This is a very reasonable direction in view of the fact that there is a great likelihood that at least a few tiny particles of the Sacred Species could still be suspended in the water.

Article III: Some Suggestions for Insuring Proper Cleanliness of the Sacred Furnishings

Although, as has been shown,[17] both the law of the Code and the laws of the liturgy insist that the sacred furnishings be kept scrupulously clean, no detail is offered regarding the method of securing the desired cleanliness; that is to say, there are no prescriptions in the general law regarding the frequency with which or the method in which the sacred furnishings are to be washed or cleaned, except of course the prescriptions of canon 1306, §2, which have just been treated. Hence, at this point, it does not appear out of place to draw up a suggested list of rules to be followed regarding the means to be used in the insuring of a proper cleanliness of the sacred furnishings. The basis for this list of rules derives from the legislation enacted in particular places, especially that of St. Charles Borromeo,[18] and from the works of some of the authors.

A. *The Sacred Vessels (chalice, paten, ciborium)*

The only prescription in the general law regarding the appearance of the sacred vessels is that the chalice and paten should be re-plated whenever a re-plating becomes necessary.[19] St. Charles Borromeo enacted the following prescriptions regarding the chalice and paten: wherever twelve priests say Mass, at least two chalices should be washed in lukewarm water every fifteen days; every six months they should be thoroughly cleaned in the following manner:

[17] Cf. *supra*, pp. 35 sqq.

[18] *Acta Ecclesiae Mediolanensis, Regulae et Instructiones de Nitore et Munditia Ecclesiarum, Altarium, Sacrorum Locorum, et Supellectilis Ecclesiasticae,* Vol. II, columns 1589-1598. (Hereafter these will be referred to as *Regulae et Instructiones.*)

[19] Cf. *supra*, pp. 65-66.

first, they are to be washed with a mild soap; then, after having been placed in the sun for fifteen minutes, they are to be thoroughly washed in a solution of lye, after which they are to be rinsed in clear water and dried.[20]

While these prescriptions of St. Charles, at least in so far as the frequency of cleaning is concerned, might be advised for churches where a large number of priests say Mass and use the sacred vessels daily, the statute of the First Synod of Fargo appears to be better suited for the average church in the United States. This Synod orders that all the sacred vessels, especially chalices, patens, and ciboria, be thoroughly purified after each use; furthermore, at least once a year, during Holy Week, they are to be thoroughly cleaned by a cleric in major orders, and the ablution poured into the sacrarium.[21] This regulation appears to be admirably suited to the needs of most parishes in the United States. In fact, it would be entirely fitting and proper that all the sacred vessels be thoroughly cleaned at least once a year. In this connection it does not seem out of place to suggest that all the metal furnishings, such as the processional cross, thuribles, candlesticks, etc., be cleaned at the same time.[22] It should be noted that the somewhat complicated process ordered by St. Charles is unnecessary in modern times; there are any number of cleansing agents which will more thoroughly and effectively serve to clean and polish gold, silver, and other metals, than the process referred to.

B. *The Sacred Linens (corporal, pall, purificator)*

The Rules and Instructions of St. Charles ordered that corporals should be changed every third week, and purificators every eight days.[23] The Diocese of Toledo prescribes that corporals be changed every three months, and that purificators should not be used for more than a week.[24] Regarding the corporals and palls, although a prescription limiting the maximum length of time for

[20] *Regulae et Instructiones,* II, col. 1593.

[21] Statutum 476.

[22] *Acta Eccl. Mediol.,* Vol. II, *Regulae et Instructiones,* col. 1594.

[23] *Ibid.,* col. 1595.

[24] *Acta et Decreta Synodi Diocesanae Toletanae Primae anno 1943* (Toledo, 1943), Statutum 192.

their use may be useful, it seems that a more wholesome rule looks to the changing of these linens as soon as they are no longer immaculately clean, that is, at the first sign of becoming soiled, or upon the appearance of the tiniest spot of dirt; furthermore, reverence and piety seem to demand that these linens be inspected by the pastor, or by any other person in charge, at least once a month.[25] Likewise, as Wapelhorst noted,[26] the prolonged use of purificators, e.g., for a month, is intolerable. A good rule to follow, and one which seems to have become custom in most places in the United States, is the changing of the purificators at least once a week, oftener if they become unusually soiled.

C. *The Vestments*

It would be difficult to suggest any rules regarding the frequency with which the linen vestments should be changed. It appears to be the common practice in the United States, as prescribed also by St. Charles,[27] to change amices weekly along with the purificators. *The Rules and Instructions* of St. Charles demanded that the albs be changed every fifteen days, the cinctures every other month.[28] In general, it can be said that the alb, and the cincture should be changed as soon as they appear to be soiled.

The outer vestments, namely, the maniple, stole, and chasuble, require cleaning but rarely. However, it is advisable to keep them covered with a clean cloth when they are not in use. It should be noted that the practice, common in many places, of turning the chasuble inside out while it is not in use is scarcely in accord with common sense; while such a procedure may possibly prevent a certain amount of dust from settling on and soiling the vestment, nevertheless it most certainly more readily wears away the embroidery or other decorations on the vestment as well as the exterior of the vestment itself.

Regarding those vestments which are used but rarely, St. Charles ordered that they be taken out of their storage place occasionally and aired out; thus was to be forestalled the formation

25 Wapelhorst, *Compendium Sacrae Liturgiae,* n. 26.

26 *Loc. cit.*

27 *Regulae et Instructiones,* II, col. 1595.

28 *Loc. cit.*

of mildew with its concurrent musty odor. The times suggested for this procedure were the months of May, September, and of some month during the winter.[29] Such a procedure was of course most necessary in climates that were very humid.

D. *The Altar Linens*

The Rules and Instructions of St. Charles regarding the altar linens appear to offer a suitable guide even for modern day practice. They prescribed that the upper or outer altar cloth should be changed once a month; the two lower cloths, four times a year. After Mass was over, the upper cloth was to be covered.[30] In this connection one should note that the altar cloths, particularly the upper cloth, may have to be changed even more frequently if they become soiled at early intervals.

[29] *Op. cit.*, II, col. 1597.
[30] *Op. cit.*, II, col. 1595-1596.

PART TWO
SECTION TWO

THE PRINCIPAL SACRED FURNISHINGS IN PARTICULAR

INTRODUCTION

In Section One of Part Two, the general law on the sacred furnishings as contained in the Code of Canon Law was explained and commented upon. It remains to consider the sacred furnishings in particular. Logically, it may be noted, such a treatment would come within the scope of Canon 1296, §3, inasmuch as that canon makes specific reference to the material and form of the sacred furnishings. However, in view of the large amount of matter included in such a treatise, it appears to be more suitable for the sake of a closer study to consider it in a separate section of the work.

Furthermore, inasmuch as it transcends the scope of this dissertation to treat of all of the sacred furnishings, it was considered best to limit the treatment to the more common or principal sacred furnishings, in particular to those which are prescribed for the celebration of Mass by the *Missal* and the *Ceremonial of Bishops*. A complete list of all the sacred furnishings necessary for cathedral and parish churches will be given at the end of this section.

In the consideration of the sacred furnishings in particular, the principal and necessary sources of the law are not the Code, but rather the liturgical books, the Decrees of the Congregation of Rites, and the liturgical writers. Hence, the following method of presentation was selected as most suitable for this treatment of the sacred furnishings: 1) Whenever possible, the prescriptions of the *Roman Missal*, the *Roman Ritual*, and the *Ceremonial of Bishops* regarding a particular sacred furnishing will be cited verbatim, and 2) an explanation and interpretation of these prescriptions will be given as derived from the Decrees of the S.R.C. and the writings of the authors.

CHAPTER IX

THE FURNISHINGS OF THE ALTAR

Article I: The Altar Cross, Candlesticks, Candles

Super Altare collocetur Crux in medio, et Candelabra saltem duo cum candelis accensis hinc et inde in utroque ejus latere.[1]

Interim dum Celebrans elevat Hostiam, accenso prius intorticio (quod non extinguitur, nisi postquam Sacerdos Sanguinem sumpserit, vel alios communicaverit, si qui erunt communicandi in Missa. . .[2]

Possunt etiam defectus occurrere in ministerio ipso, si aliquid ex requisitis ad illud desit: ut . . . si non adsint luminaria cerea . . .[3]

Supra vero in planitie altaris adsint candelabra sex argentea, si haberi possunt: sin minus ex aurichalco, aut cupro aurato nobilius fabricata, et aliquanto altiora, spectabilioraque his, quae ceteris diebus non festivis apponi solent, et super illis cerei albi, in quorum medio locabitur crux ex eodem metallo, et opere praealta, ita ut pes crucis aequet altitudinem vicinorum candelabrorum, et crux ipsa tota candelabris superemineat cum imagine sanctissimi Crucifixi, versa ad interiorem altaris faciem. Ipsa candelabra non sint omnino inter se aequalia, sed paulatim, quasi per gradus ab utroque altaris latere surgentia, ita ut ex eis altiora sint immediate hinc inde a lateribus crucis posita.[4]

Celebrante vero Episcopo, candelabra septem super altari ponantur, quo casu crux non in medio illorum, sed ante altius candelabrum in medio cereorum positum locabitur. . . .[5]

---

1 *Missale Romanum,* Tit. *Rubricae Generales Missae,* Cap. XX, *De Praeparatione Altaris, et Ornamentorum ejus.*

2 *Ibid.,* Tit. *Ritus Servandus in Celebratione Missae,* Cap. VIII, n. 6.

3 *Ibid.,* Tit. *De Defectibus in Celebratione Missarum Occurrentibus,* Cap. X, *De Defectibus in Ministerio ipso occurrentibus.*

4 *Caeremoniale Episcoporum,* Liber I, Cap. XII, n. 11.

5 *Ibid.,* n. 12.

Cetera altaria . . . habeant . . . duo saltem candelabra cum cereis, et in medio crucem cum imagine Crucifixi argenteam, vel ex aliquo metallo aut cupro aurato; scabella eorum, si fieri possit, tapetibus, vel saltem pannis cooperiantur.[6]

Dominicis diebus et aliis festis, quibus populi ab opere cessant, in ornatu altarium, sedis episcopalis, sedium Canonicorum et aliorum, eadem, sed aliquanto parcius, fieri debent, videlicet, ut paramenta non sint ita sumptuosa, coloris tamen tempori congruentis, et omnino pretiosiora illis, quae festis duplicibus minoribus, semiduplicibus, et octavis, feriis Quadragesimae, Adventus, quatuor Temporum et Vigiliarum adhibentur: quibus quidem diebus sufficient in altari quatuor candelae in candelabris; sed in festis simplicibus, et feriis per annum, duae.[7]

4. *Altare quoque, in quo* [*Episcopus*] *celebraturus est, sit mundis tobaleis et pallio condecenti ornatum, pro qualitate temporum et festorum. Nam in festis solemnibus decet in eo apponi quatuor candelabra, cum candelis accensis, et in eorum medio erit crux argentea, vel ex alia materia: in aliis festis non ita solemnioribus, et feriis, sufficiunt duo candelabra.*[8]

Si velit Episcopus celebrare die anniversaria omnium Defunctorum, vel alias quandocumque pro Defunctis, haec praeparentur et fiant: videlicet altare nullo ornatu festivo, sed simpliciter, et nullis imaginibus, sed sola cruce et sex candelabris paretur; et duo super credentia cum candelis ex cera communi . . .[9]

. . . in altari candelae ex cera communi extinctae super candelabris sint, sed nullae imagines aut alia ornamenta super altare collocentur, praeter crucem et candelabra, et haec non sint argentea.[10]

A. *The Altar Cross*

Only a cursory glance at these excerpts from the rubrics of the *Missal* and the *Ceremonial* would make it quite clear that a cross

[6] *Ibid.*, n. 16.

[7] *Ibid.*, n. 24.

[8] *Ibid.*, Cap. XXIX, n. 4.

[9] *Ibid.*, Liber II, Cap. XI, n. 1.

[10] *Ibid.*, Cap. XXV, *Praeparanda pro officio ferriae sextae in Parasceve*, n. 2.

is to be placed on the altar for the celebration of Mass. Commentaries on the liturgy usually consider this cross to be the most important of all the altar furnishings.[11] The cross occupies the most conspicuous place on the altar, the very center. The altar should be so furnished and arranged that attention is always and foremost drawn towards the cross. As the *Ceremonial* states, the cross should be higher than the candlesticks; the base of the cross should be equal in height to the candlesticks, while the image on the cross should exceed the height of the candlesticks.[12]

This cross should be large enough to be seen by the celebrating priest and by the people of the congregation. The S.R.C. as well as the Roman Pontiff himself have reprobated the practice of using a small cross placed on the tabernacle or on a card in the middle of the altar.[13] During Mass, the cross should always remain exposed and visible; it is not to be veiled except during Passiontide.[14]

This furnishing is not to be a simple cross but a crucifix, that is to say, it should have an image of the Crucified, which should be turned towards the celebrant.[15] The *Ceremonial* directs that the crucifix should be made of the same material as the candlesticks, namely of gold, of silver, or of brass, at least for the greater feast days;[16] however, it also admits the use of other metal[17] or of other material.[18] Hence the liturgical writers conclude that the

[11] L. O'Connell, *The Book of Ceremonies,* p. 9; J. O'Connell, *The Celebration of Mass* (3 vols., Milwaukee: Bruce, 1940-1941) I, 247; Anson, *Churches,* p. 104. This last author notes that the cross is perhaps the least ancient of all the furnishings of the altar; there seems to have been no law making its use obligatory before the Reformation period.

[12] *Caeremoniale Episcoporum.* Lib. I, Cap. XII, n. 11.

[13] S.R.C., *Dubiorum.,* 17 sept. 1822 ad 7—*Decr. Auth.,* n. 2621: *Rossanen.,* 16 iun. 1633 ad 1—*Decr. Auth.,* n. 1270; Benedictus XIV, litt. encycl. *Accepimus,* 16 iul. 1746—*BRT,* Vol. II, col. 111-115; the title of the discussion is given as: *De retinenda Crucifixi Salvatoris Imagine, palam et visibiliter super Altaribus.*

[14] S.R.C., *Molinen.,* 12 sept. 1857, ad XI—*Decr. Auth.,* n. 3059.

[15] *Caeremoniale Episcoporum,* Lib. I, Cap. XII, n. 11.

[16] *Loc. cit.*

[17] *Ibid.,* n. 16.

[18] *Ibid.,* Cap. XXIX, n. 4.

rubrics do not specify any particular material for the cross. Accordingly it could not be said that there is any prohibition against the use of crosses made of wood.[19] It seems to be preferred that for more solemn days the cross be made of a precious or semi-precious metal, while for the penitential seasons and Requiems it be made of less precious metal or of wood.[20]

The directions of the *Ceremonial* demand a variation in the kind of cross which is used, depending upon the feast or the season. It appears that this practice is not commonly observed, at least in the United States; most churches have one set of candlesticks, either of metal or of wood, which are used for all functions and for all days.

The directions of the *Ceremonial* not only state that the altar cross should be made of the same material as the candlesticks, but also that the former should be executed in the same style of workmanship as the latter.[21] This is a detail which is not infrequently disregarded.

From the words of the *Missal* and the *Ceremonial* it is quite clear that the crucifix should stand on the altar, that is to say, on the table or *mensa* itself, or on a gradine, if there is one, and always on the same level as the candlesticks. This naturally proves somewhat inconvenient in most of the churches in the United States because of the fact that the tabernacle is usually on the main altar of the church. Strict observance of the rubrics would demand that the cross be placed on the altar behind the tabernacle. It is never permissible to place it in front of the tabernacle.[22]

A very satisfactory solution to this problem, when the *mensa* is too narrow for the cross to stand behind the tabernacle, is to use a cross, similar to a processional cross, the shaft of which is attached to the back of the altar.[23] In fact, St. Charles Borromeo directed that the cross of the high altar of the church be the pro-

[19] Anson, *Churches,* p. 106.

[20] Anson, *loc. cit.;* L. O'Connell, *The Book of Ceremonies,* p. 9.

[21] Lib. I, Cap. XII, n. 11.

[22] S.R.C., *Ordinis FF, Minorum Provinciae Portugalliae,* 11 iun. 1904 ad 2 *Decr. Auth.,* n. 4136.

[23] Anson, *Churches,* p. 106.

cessional cross, especially when the presence of a tabernacle made it impossible to have the cross standing on the altar.[24]

Another solution, commonly offered by the authors, is to suspend the cross above the altar between the candlesticks.[25] This practice of suspending the cross above the altar, commonly referred to as the "hanging crucifix," appears to have gained considerable popularity, at least in the United States, within the last fifteen or twenty years. In many quarters an altar with a "hanging crucifix" is frequently referred to as a "liturgical altar;" the use of the first term seems to imply that an altar which has the cross suspended above it, rather than standing on it or on the tabernacle, is correct liturgically. As has just been noted, the rubrics of the *Missal* and of the *Ceremonial* direct quite clearly that the cross is to stand on the altar; these liturgical books made no mention of the cross being suspended above the altar.

Those who advocate, or at least tolerate, the use of the hanging crucifix, apparently base their opinion on one Decree of the S.R.C., namely, Decree 4136.[26] For the sake of clarity, it seems best to quote that part of the decree which is apropos. It was asked:

> II. *An Crux cum imagine Crucifixi, in medio Altaris inter candelabra collocanda, etiam in Altari, ubi Sanctissimum asservatur, collocari possit immediate ante eius tabernaculum; aut super ipsum, vel in postica eius parte collocari debeat?*

The response of the S.R.C. was:

> *Ad. II. Crux collocetur inter candelabra, nunquam ante ostiolum tabernaculi. Potest etiam collocari super ipsum tabernaculum, non autem in throno ubi exponitur Sanctissimum Eucharistiae Sacramentum.*

First of all, it should be noted that the import of the question and the reply indicate that the questioner was faced with the problem mentioned above, namely, an altar with a tabernacle so constructed that it was impossible to place the cross on the altar as the rubrics direct.

[24] *Acta Eccl. Mediol., Instructionum supellectilis Ecclesiasticae* Liber II, *De Cruce,* Vol. II, col. 1554.

[25] Anson, *Churches,* p. 106; J. O'Connell, *The Celebration of Mass,* I, 247.

[26] Cf. *supra,* fn.; Anson, *op. cit., loc. cit.;* J. O'Connell, *op. cit., loc. cit.*

Secondly, it appears that the S.R.C. overlooked that part of the query which seemed to call for an answer to the question whether the cross may be suspended above the altar, namely *"in postica eius parte."* The response seems rather to demand that the cross be placed on the altar itself.

Thirdly, the word *"collocari,"* as used in the Decree, does not mean "to be hung" or "to be suspended," but rather "to be placed" or "to be set." It is difficult to interpret the wording of the decree in any manner except that it states that the cross is to be *placed* on the altar.

A very broad and carefree translation of the words *"Potest etiam collocari super ipsum tabernaculum"* could lead one to conclude that the cross may be suspended above the tabernacle, at least in such cases when the altar construction makes it impossible for the cross to be placed on the altar as the rubrics demand.

While this problem of the placing of the cross on the altar can easily arise wtih regard to poorly constructed altars already in existence, it can scarcely figure in reference to new altars. Hence, obedience to the rubrics will demand that, in the designing of new altars, ample provision be made for the placing of the cross in the proper place, that is, on the altar.

From the Decree of the S.R.C. as just cited, it is evident that the cross is not to be placed on the throne used for the exposition of the Blessed Sacrament. However, it appears to be permissible to place the cross on the tabernacle itself, provided that it is not placed on precisely the same spot that is used for exposition.[27]

The S.R.C. admits of two exceptions to the rubric that a cross must be placed on the altar for the celebration of Mass. First, if the principal feature of the altar piece or the reredos is a figure of the Crucified, no other cross is needed.[28] J. O'Connell, however, is of the opinion that even in such a case it is better to place a cross on the altar.[29] The second exception obtains when Mass is celebrated *coram Sanctissimo;* on such occasions the cross may

[27] S.R.C., *Cuneen.*, 2 iun. 1883, ad III—*Decr. Auth.*, n. 3576.
[28] S.R.C., *Rossanen.*, 16 iun. 1633, ad 2—*Decr. Auth.*, n. 1270.
[29] *Op. cit.*, I, 247.

remain in its proper place or be removed in accord with local custom.[30]

B. *The Candlesticks*

The rubrics of the *Missal* require at least two candlesticks on the altar for the celebration of Mass.[31] The directions of the *Ceremonial* require seven for a Pontifical Mass,[32] six for a solemn Mass or for Masses on the more solemn days,[33] four for the less solemn feasts, and two for simple feasts or ferials.[34] It further directs that all the altars in the church are to have at least two candlesticks.[35]

On the high or main altar there are to be six candlesticks, similar in design to and made of the same material as the altar cross, namely of gold, of silver, or of brass for feast days, and of less precious metal or of wood for penitential seasons and Requiems. Ordinarily, except in cathedral churches, the high altar will have six large candlesticks, and in front of these two or four small candlesticks. The latter, being used for private Masses, and hence not forming part of the normal furnishing of the altar, should be removed immediately after Mass.[36] In like manner, the candlesticks which are placed on the altar for Benediction, or for the Exposition of the Blessed Sacrament and for other devotions, should be removed immediately after such devotions.

These six candlesticks should be arranged on either side of the cross, that is, three on each side and on the same plane as the cross. In cathedral churches, a seventh candlestick will be a part of the ordinary furnishing of the main altar; this is required for a

[30] S.R.C., *Aquen.*, 2 sept. 1741, ad I—*Decr. Auth.*, n. 2365. Cf. also Benedictus XIV, litt. encyc. *Accepimus, Quarto loco.*

[31] Tit. *Rub. Gen.*, Cap. XX.

[32] Lib. I, Cap. XII, n. 12.

[33] *Ibid.*, n. 11.

[34] *Ibid.*, n. 24.

[35] *Ibid.*, n. 16.

[36] Fortescue, *The Ceremonies of the Roman Rite Described* (7th ed. revised and augmented by J. O'Connell, London: Burns, Oates and Washbourne, 1947), p. 7; Anson, *Churches*, p. 108.

Pontifical Mass by the bishop of the diocese. It will also be required on the occasions when the bishop pontificates in other churches.[37] In this case the seventh candlestick is to be taller than the others and should be placed behind the altar cross.[38]

The *Ceremonial* directs that these six main candlesticks are not to be of the same height; they should increase in height, rising in echelon from the outside to the center so that the tallest are nearest the altar cross. However, modern custom, approved by the S.R.C., appears to prefer that these candlesticks be of the same height.[39]

For private Masses, when only two candlesticks are required, a third candlestick is to be prepared on the epistle side of the altar;[40] this candlestick, when used, is generally a bracket fixed to the wall.[41] It should not be placed on the altar itself but on the credence table, on the floor, or in a bracket, as has just been described. Although custom appears to have dispensed with the "elevation candle," so the S.R.C. has decreed,[42] it is still within the power of the ordinary to order the observance of this rubric.[43]

Anson's work contains an interesting footnote inserted by H. A. Reinhold regarding the use of this candle:

> There is no reason why in this eucharistic age this *Sanctus* candle should not be reintroduced, where it has been neglected. Its reintroduction has everywhere been accompanied by a great reverence and closer participation in the sacred mysteries by the faithful.—H.A.R.[44]

The proper place for the candlesticks seems to be on the *mensa* of the altar. However, if the altar has gradines, the candlesticks

[37] *Caeremoniale Episcoporum,* Lib. I, cap. XII, n. 12.

[38] *Loc. cit.;* S.R.C., *Placentina,* 19 maii 1607 ad 8—*Decr. Auth.,* n. 235.

[39] *Caeremoniale Episcoporum,* Lib. I, Cap. XII, n. 11; S.R.C., *Briocen.,* 21 iul. 1855 ad 7—*Decr. Auth.,* n. 3035.

[40] *Missale Romanum,* Tit. *Ritus Servandus in Celebratione Missae,* Cap. VIII, n. 6.

[41] J. O'Connell, *The Celebration of Mass,* III, 249.

[42] *Resolutionis Dubiorum,* 9 iun. 1899, ad 2—*Decr. Auth.,* n. 4029.

[43] S.R.C., *Ordinis Fratrum Minorum Provinciae Anglicae,* 29 iul. 1904, ad 6—*Decr. Auth.,* n. 4141.

[44] *Churches,* p. 108.

may be placed on them.[45] This seems to be the accepted practice in many places in the United States. It is not permissible to have the candlesticks standing on the floor on either side of the altar, or to have them attached to the wall. Likewise, branched candlesticks are not allowed to be used as the proper furnishing of the altar for the celebration of Mass. The candlesticks which are prescribed for Mass are presumed to be single candlesticks.[46]

The candlesticks should not ordinarily be covered with veils or cloths to keep the dust from them even during the seasons of Advent and Lent.[47] This ruling must be observed at least during the time that Mass is being celebrated.[48] However, a later decree states that covering gold candlesticks with a veil, either during or outside of the time of Mass, may be tolerated except on the more solemn days.[49]

C. *Candles*

1. Number

The usual interpretation of the rubrics of the *Missal* and the *Ceremonial* regarding the number of candles necessary for Mass is that at least two must be lighted for a Low Mass, while six are required for a Solemn Mass. Liturgical writers[50] hold that for a strictly private Mass of any priest, even if he be a prelate, or the vicar general, below the rank of bishop, only two candles are to be used. This is substantiated by several decrees of the S.R.C.[51]

[45] S.R.C., *Briocen.*, 21 iul. 1855, ad 7—*Decr. Auth.*, n. 3035; *Lucana,* 5 dec. 1891, ad 2—*Decr. Auth.*, n. 3759.

[46] S.R.C., *Cameracen.*, 16 sept. 1865, ad 1 et 4—*Decr. Auth.*, n. 3137.

[47] S.R.C., *Collen.*, 31 aug. 1872—*Decr. Auth.*, n. 3266.

[48] S.R.C., *Molinen.*, 12 sept. 1857, ad II—*Decr. Auth.*, n. 3059.

[49] S.R.C., *Cameracen.*, 16 sept. 1865, ad 2—*Decr. Auth.*, n. 3137.

[50] J. O'Connell, *The Celebration of Mass,* I, 250; L. O'Connell, *The Book of Ceremonies,* p. 12; Fortescue, *Ceremonies of the Roman Rite Described,* p. 7; Wapelhorst, *Compendium Sacrae Liturgiae,* n. 22; Cappello, *De Sacramentis,* I, n. 727.

[51] *Castri Durantis,* 7 aug., 1627—*Decr. Auth.*, n. 441; *Cusetina.*, 5 iul. 1631—*Decr. Auth.*, n. 567; *Neopolitana.*, 26 ian. 1658—*Decr. Auth.*, n. 1051; *Decretum.*, 27 sept. 1659—*Decr. Auth.*, n. 1131; *Tiburtina.*, 7 sept. 1850—*Decr. Auth.*, n. 2984.

It must be observed that for other Low Masses, such as are not strictly private, more than two candles are permitted. Such Masses would be: a) Conventual Masses, which even apart from being a sung or chanted Mass, can be considered solemn with reference to the number of candles to be employed;[52] b) parochial or similar Masses, for example, that of a religious community, which cannot be sung since no choir is available, at least for Sundays and feast days;[53] c) Masses which replace sung or solemn Masses on occasions of very special solemnity, for example, the First Communion Day in a parish.[54]

For sung Masses the ordinary practice, at least in the United States, is to light six candles. The liturgical writers generally advise that six candles are to be used at least on the more solemn days and on special occasions, and at least four on other days.[55] The Decrees of the S.R.C. contain very few regulations regarding the number of candles to be used for sung Masses. One decree allows the lighting of more candles on feast days.[56] It does prescribe however that, for Requiem Masses that are sung, at least four candles are to be lit.[57]

Inasmuch as for the most part in most of the parishes in the United States the sung Mass takes the place of the Solemn Mass, it seems that a safe and plausible rule to follow is the prescription given by the *Ceremonial* regarding the number of candles to be used for solemn Masses, namely: for Masses celebrated on Sundays and feast days, six candles; for Masses celebrated on other days, four candles are sufficient; for Masses celebrated on simple days and ferials, two candles.[58]

[52] S.R.C., *Ordinis Minoris Capuccinorum S. Francisci,* 7 dec. 1888, ad 7—*Decr. Auth.*, n. 3697.

[53] S.R.C., *Molinen.*, 12 sept. 1857, ad 9—*Decr. Auth.*, n. 3059; *Northantonien.*, 6 febr. 1858—*Decr. Auth.* n. 3065.

[54] Cappello, *De Sacramentis,* I, n. 727.

[55] L. O'Connell, *The Book of Ceremonies,* p. 12; J. O'Connell, *The Celebration of Mass,* III, 250.

[56] S.R.C., *Nullius Dioecesis Piscien.*, 6 maii 1873, ad 2—*Decr. Auth.*, n. 1470.

[57] S.R.C., *Briocen.*, 12 aug. 1854, ad 7—*Decr. Auth.*, n. 3029.

[58] *Caeremoniale Episcoporum,* Lib. I, Cap. XII, n. 11; n. 24.

For the low Mass of a bishop ordinarily four candles are to be used at least for solemn feasts; on other days two are sufficient.[59] He is also directed to use seven candles for Solemn non-Requiem Masses as well as for Low Masses of Ordination in churches and public oratories.[60] For Solemn Requiem Masses at which the bishop is the celebrant, six candles, not seven, are prescribed by the *Ceremonial.*[61]

For private Benediction of the Blessed Sacrament at least six candles must be lighted on the altar.[62] For Solemn Benediction at least twelve candles should be used.[63] However, the S.R.C. in 1910 gave permission for public exposition in poor churches with only six candles upon the previous permission of the ordinary.[64] At the present time, however, it appears that the S.R.C. is still most solicitous that at least twelve candles be used for public exposition; in 1941 it decreed that it was not proper to use only eight candles for public exposition, except in cases where candles could not be obtained; even then it suggested that the deficiency be corrected through the use of other means, even of electric lights.[65] Twenty candles are required for exposition during Forty Hours' Devotion.[66]

2. Quality

The liturgical writers appear to be unanimous in their opinion

[59] *Caeremoniale Episcoporum,* Lib. I, Cap. XXXIX, n. 4.

[60] *Caeremoniale Episcoporum,* Lib. I, Cap. XII, n. 12; S.R.C., *Marsorum.,* 12 nov. 1831, ad 8—*Decr. Auth.,* n. 2682.

[61] Liber II, Cap. XI, n. 1.

[62] S.R.C., *Marnien.,* 15 mart. 1698—*Decr. Auth.,* n. 1992.

[63] S.R.C., *Aturen. et Aquen.,* 8 febr. 1879—*Decr. Auth.,* n. 3480.

[64] *Tunquen.,* 30 iul. 1910, ad 4—*Decr. Auth.,* n. 4257.

[65] S.R.C., *Dioecesium Brasiliensium,* 14 febr. 1941—ad III; this decree is contained in *Collectio Decretorum ad Sacram Liturgiam Spectantium ab anno 1927 ad annum 1946* (ed. 2a, Roma: Edizione Liturgiche, 1947). (This work will be cited as *Coll. Decr.;* the number given will be that which is assigned to the decree in the work itself.) For this reference, *Coll. Decr.,* n. 78.

[66] *Instructio Clementina,* S.R.C. *Decr. Auth.,* Vol. IV, pp. 1-138, and in particular pp. 22-26, VI.

that the *"cereus"* required by the directions of the *Missal* and the *Ceremonial* is a candle of pure beeswax.[67] Although the S.R.C. has given a ruling that the paschal candle and the two candles required for Mass be of pure beeswax at least in *"maxima parte"* and that all other candles which are to be placed on the altar be of pure beeswax at least in major or notable quantity, it would be better if all the candles on the altar were made of pure beeswax. In fact, this response of the S.R.C. was given because of the great difficulty in either obtaining pure beeswax or in obtaining candles which were not mixed with some foreign material. The S.R.C. has shown itself very lenient in this matter when particular circumstances make it difficult to obtain candles of beeswax; thus it permitted one ordinary for a period of five years to use candles that were only thirty per cent beeswax.[68]

It can hardly be said that any such extraordinary circumstances exist in the United States at the present time. One hundred per cent beeswax candles are obtainable from nearly any church goods dealer in the country. Likewise it cannot be said that the cost of such candles is prohibitive. Locally[69] the price for candles of 100% beeswax is $1.80 per pound; 60%, $1.60 per pound; 51%, $1.56 per pound. It seems that such a small difference in price should not deter rectors of churches from obtaining candles which are not only strictly in accord with the rubrics but also are considered to be the best.

Many tests show that the 100% beeswax candle will burn 30% to 50% longer than the 51% beeswax candle.[70]

However, common practice and the liturgical writers confirm the use of candles made from beeswax *"in maxima parte."* Decree 4147 of the S.R.C. leaves the determination of what is to be

[67] Cf. *supra*, pp. 78-79; Anson, *Churches*, p. 111; Cappello, *De Sacramentis*, I, n. 727; Fortescue, *Ceremonies of the Roman Rite Described*, p. 7; Gasparri, *De SS. Eucharistia*, n. 783; J. O'Connell, *The Celebration of Mass*, I, 249; Wapelhorst, *Compendium Sacrae Liturgiae*, n. 22. S.R.C., *Purium Dioecesium*, 14 dec. 1904—*Decr. Auth.* n. 4147.

[68] S.R.C. *Tridentina*, 18 iun. 1940—*Coll. Decr.*, n. 66.

[69] I.e., in Washington, D. C.

[70] Collins, *The Church Edifice and Its Appointments* (Westminster, Md.: Newman Bookshop, 1946) hereafter cited *The Church Edifice*), p. 123.

understood by *"maxima parte"* and *"in maiori vel notabili quantitate"* to the local ordinaries. In most places it appears that *"maxima parte"* is taken to be 60-75% beeswax; *"maiori vel notabili quantitate,"* 51% beeswax.[71]

Except on Good Friday and for Requiem Masses, when unbleached candles are prescribed,[72] white or bleached candles are to be used.[73]

S.R.C. 4147 also makes it clear that no candles are permitted on the altar if they are not at least partly beeswax. Several other decrees have repeatedly forbidden the use on or within the ambit of the altar, either for cultual purposes, that is, to meet the requirements of the liturgy, or for ornamentation, of candles made from materials other than beeswax, such as paraffin, stearine, or tallow.[74]

Imitation or dummy candles, that is, painted metal or wooden tubes which contain small candles that are pushed to the opening under the pressure of a spring have been declared legitimate by the S.R.C.[75] Liturgical writers, however, bewail the use of such imitations as undignified and unbecoming.[76]

The use of electric lights on or near the altar in place of or in addition to the candles prescribed for Mass, Benediction, or Exposition of the Blessed Sacrament has been forbidden by the S.R.C.[77] The Congregation is most insistent that all attempts at

[71] Anson, *Churches,* p. 111; Van der Stappen, *Sacra Liturgia* (3 ed., 5 vols. Mechliniae, 1911-1915), III, 90; Fortescue notes that the bishops of England and Wales determined upon 65% as *maxima parte,* and 25% as *maiori vel notabili parte.* (*Op. cit.,* p. 7.)

[72] *Caeremoniale Episcoporum,* Liber II, Cap. XI, n. 1; Cap. XXV, n. 2.

[73] *Ibid.,* Liber I, Cap. XII, n. 11.

[74] S.R.C., *Massilien.,* 16 sept. 1843—*Decr. Auth.,* n. 2865; *Carolinopolitana,* 10 dec. 1857—*Decr. Auth.,* n. 3063; *Sanctimonialium Perpetuae Adorationis SS. Sacramenti,* 27 iun. 1868—*Decr. Auth.,* n. 3173; *Policastren.,* 4 sept. 1875, ad III.—*Decr. Auth.* 3376; *Tunquen.,* 30 iul. 1910, ad 5—*Decr. Auth.,* n. 4257.

[75] *Societatis Iesu,* 11 maii 1878, ad 13—*Decr. Auth.,* n. 3448.

[76] Anson, *Churches,* p. 111; J. O'Connell, *The Celebration of Mass,* I, 249.

[77] *Novarcen.,* 29 nov. 1901—*Decr. Auth.,* n. 4086; *Nacheten.,* 16 maii 1902 —*Decr. Auth.,* n. 4097; *Declaratio Decretorum de Luce Electrica,* 22 nov.

anything theatrical be entirely avoided. The most recent Decree (n. 4322, of 1914) deserves to be quoted:

> *Summa autem Decretorum haec est: Lux electrica vetita est, non solum una cum candelis ex cera super altaria (4097), sed etiam loco candelarum vel lampadum, quae coram SSmo vel Reliquiis Sanctorum praescriptae sunt. Pro aliis ecclesiae locis et ceteris casibus, illuminatio electrica, ad prudens Ordinarii judicium, permittitur, dummodo in omnibus servetur gravitas, quam sanctitas loci et dignitas sacrae Liturgiae postulant. (3859, 4206, 4210) Nec licet, tempore expositionis privatae vel publicae, interiorem partem ciborii cum lampadibus electricis in ipsa parte interiori collocatis illuminare, ut SSma Eucharistia melius a fidelibus conspici possit. (4275)*

Article II: Tabernacle Furnishings

A. *Tabernacle Lamp*

> Canon 1271.—*Coram tabernaculo, in quo sanctissimum Sacramentum asservatur, una saltem lampas diu noctuque continenter luceat, nutrienda oleo olivarum vel cera apum; ubi vero oleum olivarum haberi nequeat, Ordinarii loci prudentiae permittitur ut aliis oleis commutetur, quantum fieri potest, vegetalibus.*
>
> *Sed in primus . . .* [*sacrista*] *diligentissime curabit, ut et, quae ad sacrosanctae Eucharistiae cultum et honorem spectant, nitide conserventur, locusque, seu tabernaculum, ubi custoditur, diligentissime et fides clavibus obseretur; lampades circa illam perpetuo ardeant; . . .*[78]
>
> *Lampades . . . in primis adhibendae sunt ante altare, vel locum, ubi asservatur Ss. Sacramentum, et ante altare majus, quibus in locis lampadarios pensiles esse decet, plures sustintentes lampades, ex quibus, qui ante altare majus erit, tres ad minus: qui ante Sacramentum, saltem quinque lucernas habeat . . . Ante Ss. Sacramentum, si non omnes, ad minus tres accensae tota die adsint.*[79]
>
> *Coram eo una saltem lampas diu noctuque continenter luceat, nutrienda oleo olivarum vel cera apum; ubi vero oleum olivarum haberi nequeat, Ordinarii loci prudentiae*

1907—*Decr. Auth.*, n. 4206; *Angelopolitana*, 17 ian. 1908—*Decr. Auth.*, n. 4210; *Decretum de Luce Electrica super altare non adhibenda*, 24 iun. 1914—*Decr. Auth.*, n. 4322.

[78] *Caeremoniale Episcoporum*, Lib. I, Cap. VI, n. 2.

[79] *Ibid.*, Cap. XII, n. 17.

permittitur ut aliis oleis commutetur, quantum fieri potest, vegetabilibus.[80]

The sanctuary lamp is a relatively recent innovation. There is no evidence that lamps were lit in honor of the Blessed Sacrament before the twelfth century. During the middle ages lamps were hung around the ciborium and burned before the relics of saints. A certain Eustace, Abbott of Fleury, went through England and France preaching that there should be in every church a burning lamp or some other perpetual light before the Lord's Body. However, it appears that it was not until the sixteenth century that a lamp was considered as strictly obligatory.[81]

The *Ceremonial,* which directs that such lamps be burned before the Blessed Sacrament, was issued just in the 17th century (1600).

The directions of the *Ceremonial* order that more than one lamp burn before the Blessed Sacrament, mentioning three as the minimum.[82] The authors interpret this to mean that, if more than one lamp is used, an odd number should be used.[83] The Code and the Ritual, however, speak of only one lamp as being necessary.[84]

It appears that until the time of the Code, only olive oil was considered the proper fuel for sanctuary lamps. This is evident from the fact that the S.R.C. granted permission for the use of other oils for this purpose, including a mixture of olive oil and beeswax, and then only as late as 1908 was any permission granted for the use of beeswax, and then only with the prudent consent of the ordinary.[85] The use of an electric light in place of an olive oil or beeswax lamp was permitted only with the prudent permission of the ordinary, and as a last resort, *"ultimo loco."*[86] This ruling was issued as a war-time measure during World War I. The S.R.C.

80 *Rituale Romanum,* Tit. IV, Cap. 1, *De Sanctissimo Eucharistiae Sacramento,* n. 6.

81 Anson, *Churches,* p. 112.

82 Lib. I, Cap. XII, n. 17.

83 Anson, *Churches,* p. 112.

84 *Loc. cit.*

85 S.R.C., *Plurium Dioecesium,* 9 iul. 1864—*Decr. Auth.,* n. 3121; *Carcassonen.,* 8 nov. 1907—*Decr. Auth.,* n. 4205; *Romana,* 27 nov. 1908—*Decr. Auth.,* n. 4230.

86 S.R.C., *Decretum de lampade coram sanctissimo Sacramento,* 23 febr.

issued a similar decree during World War II, giving the same permission under the same condition.[87]

The rubrics neither order nor suggest the proper color for the sanctuary lamp. Liturgists recommend that it be white.[88] The S.R.C., however, has answered that the use of various colored lamps, red, blue, and green being mentioned specifically, is permissible.[89] However, as one writer notes, if there are other lamps in the church, it is better that they be provided with a glass of a color different from that used before the Blessed Sacrament.[90]

Neither the rubrics nor the Decrees of the S.R.C. make any mention of the size or the shape of the sanctuary lamp. It may be suspended from the ceiling on chains and pulleys for convenience in replenishing and cleaning, or it may be placed on a stand near the tabernacle. However, it must be placed before and within the ambit of the altar on which the Blessed Sacrament is reserved.[91] It is not to be placed on the *mensa* or on a gradine of the altar; likewise it is not to be placed immediately above the altar.[92]

B. *Tabernacle Veil*

> *Hoc autem tabernaculum conopaeo decenter opertum atque ab omni alia re vacuum, in Altari majori vel in alio . . . sit collocatum.*[93]

1. Necessity

Although the statement from the *Ritual* just cited is the only mention which the liturgical books make regarding the tabernacle veil, liturgical writers are most insistent that such a veil is obligatory for any tabernacle which contains the Blessed Sacrament. Thus Anson states that it "is absolutely obligatory";[94] L. O'Connell says that "the tabernacle in which the Blessed Sacrament is

1916—*Decr. Auth.*, n. 4334.

[87] *Urbis et Orbis,* 13 mart. 1942—*Coll. Decr.*, n. 86.

[88] Anson, *Churches,* p. 112.

[89] S.R.C., *Cuneen.*, 2 iun. 1883, ad 5—*Decr. Auth.*, n. 3576.

[90] Anson, *Churches,* p. 112.

[91] S.R.C., *Cuneen.*, 2 iun. 1883, ad 4—*Decr. Auth.*, n. 3576.

[92] S.R.C., *Romana,* 20 iun. 1899, ad 6—*Decr. Auth.*, n. 4035.

[93] *Rituale Romanum,* Tit. IV, Cap. 1, n. 6.

[94] *Churches,* p. 94.

reserved must be covered with a veil."[95] Cappello states: "*Necesse est ut* CONOPEO, *seu velo ad instar tentorii operiatur.*"[96] One could scarcely deduce such a strict obligation from the words of the *Ritual.* Several decrees of the S.R.C., however, appear to make it more mandatory. Thus in response to the question, "Whether the tabernacle in which the Blessed Sacrament is reserved should be covered with a veil as the *Ritual* states?" the S.R.C. answered "*Affirmative.*"[97] In another decree it ruled: . . .*Tabernaculum tegendum est Conopeo, iuxta praescriptum Ritualis Romani.*[98]

The fact that the tabernacle is made of precious metal or is decorated very artistically is not considered a legitimate excuse for not using the veil. The S.R.C. has ruled that even in such cases the tabernacle must be covered with the veil.[99] Even the consideration of a long-standing custom cannot be advanced as an argument against the use of the tabernacle veil. The S.R.C. has explicitly ruled that such a custom cannot be maintained and that the *Ritual* is to be observed.[100]

From these constant and continued rulings of the S.R.C. it is quite manifest that the tabernacle in which the Blessed Sacrament is reserved must be covered with a veil. None of the commentaries on the liturgy and no canonists advance any reason for the strict observance of this rubric. Neither does the S.R.C. explain its demand for such strict observance. The Code states simply that the tabernacle is to be becomingly decorated in accord with the laws of the liturgy.[101]

The ultimate reason for the strict observance of this rubric probably is contained in the fact that the tabernacle veil "is the only sure indication of the presence of the Blessed Sacrament on the altar."[102] This can be deduced from the fact that the veil is the only furnishing which is strictly demanded to adorn the tabernacle

95 *The Book of Ceremonies,* p. 6.
96 *De Sacramentis,* I, n. 329.
97 *Briocen.,* 21 iul. 1855, ad 10—*Decr. Auth.,* n. 3035.
98 *Sancti Iacobi de Cile,* 28 apr. 1866—*Decr. Auth.,* n. 3150.
99 *Auxitana,* 7 aug. 1888—*Decr. Auth.,* n. 3520.
100 *Dubium,* 1 iul. 1904—*Decr. Auth.,* n. 4137.
101 Canon 1269, §2.
102 L. O'Connell, *The Book of Ceremonies,* p. 583.

where the Blessed Sacrament is reserved. It is true that most people consider the tabernacle lamp as the sign that the Blessed Sacrament is present. However, the lamp is not a sure indication, at least not in larger churches where several lamps may be seen in front of several altars. Furthermore, the *Adnotationes* to the Instruction of the Congregation of the Sacraments make the following observation:

> 12. It is left to the prudent initiative of the pastors to see to it that especially in churches situated in large cities, the altar where the tabernacle which contains the Blessed Sacrament is, be easily distinguished by the faithful from all other altars, by some certain and conspicuous mark, for the sake of avoiding irreverence toward it . . .[103]

If the tabernacle veil is accepted as the only sure indication that the Blessed Sacrament is reserved in the tabernacle, then its use appears imperative in the fulfillment of the requirements of the Instruction just cited. Furthermore, if it is accepted as such an indication, then the reason for the law becomes clear.

The only time the S.R.C. has permitted the omission of the tabernacle veil was when respect and reverence for the Blessed Sacrament demanded it. The facts of the situation were these: insects of various kinds hid themselves underneath the veil, so that very often when the tabernacle door was opened the insects entered into the tabernacle itself. The S.R.C. left the matter to the prudent judgment of the ordinary.[104] From this Cappello concludes that, whenever it is morally impossible to use the veil, one may legitimately forego its use.[105]

2. Form

The word which as used in the *Ritual* has been translated as veil is *conopeum*. The Latin equivalent of veil, *velum,* is not used in the Decrees of the S.R.C. to refer to the tabernacle veil; the word *conopeum* is the only word used. A more proper and exact trans-

[103] *AAS,* XXI (1929), 642; translation from Bouscaren, *The Canon Law Digest* (2 vols. and *Supplement* through 1948, Milwaukee: Bruce, 1934, 1943, 1949), I, 367.

[104] S.R.C. *Vicariatus Apostolici utriusque Guineae,* 27 iul. 1878—*Decr. Auth.,* n. 3456.

[105] *De Sacramentis,* I, n. 329.

lation of *conopeum* would be "canopy." Anson observes that *conopeum* literally is a mosquito net, that is to say, a veil that entirely envelops the tabernacle.[106] The *Ritual* itself[107] speaks of the tabernacle being covered *(opertum)* with the veil; likewise the S.R.C. uses the word to cover, i.e., *tegendum.*[108] Hence the tabernacle veil or canopy should be such as to cover or envelop the entire tabernacle;[109] it should be in the form of a tent, so that it covers the whole tabernacle, on the top and at the sides.[110]

From this requirement it is evident that the mere hanging of veils or curtains in front of the doors of the tabernacle does not meet the requirements of the law.[111] Neither can metal plaques or painted pictures of Eucharistic symbols, or of the Holy Name, or of the Blessed Virgin, be used to replace the tabernacle veil.[112]

There is a divergence of opinion among the writers regarding those tabernacles which are so constructed that a veil of the kind required by the law cannot possibly be fitted over them. Anson,[113] Cappello[114] and Cavanaugh[115] hold that in such cases the faulty construction of the tabernacle makes it physically impossible to fulfill the law and that inasmuch as the S.R.C. has ruled that curtains do not meet the requirements of the law, not even these need be used. Anson's remarks are interesting:

> Such tabernacles are not "tabernacles"—i.e., tents—in the strict meaning of the word, but are really "sacrament houses" erected on the altar: a survival of an epoch before existing legislation. They are best regarded as "period

---

106 *Churches,* p. 94.

107 *Loc. cit.*

108 Cf. Decrees nn. 3035; 3150; *supra,* p. 96.

109 Anson, *Churches,* p. 94.

110 L. O'Connell, *The Book of Ceremonies,* p. 6; Cappello, *De Sacramentis,* I, n. 329.

111 S.R.C., *Mexicana.,* 10 sept. 1898, ad 1—*Decr. Auth.,* n. 4000.

112 *Loc. cit.*

113 *Churches,* p. 94.

114 *De Sacramentis,* I, n. 329.

115 *The Reservation of the Blessed Sacrament* (The Catholic University of America Canon Law Studies, n. 40, Washington, D. C.: The Catholic University of America, 1927), p. 59.

> pieces" and treated with the respect that their age deserves![116]

L. O'Connell[117] and Collins,[118] on the contrary, hold that when it is impossible to put a proper veil on the tabernacle the use of a veil in front of the door is better than no veil at all. This latter opinion appears to be more in accord with the spirit of the law, at least when one considers the veil to be the only sure indication of the presence of the Blessed Sacrament.

The actual shape of the veil will depend on the shape of the tabernacle. No particular material is prescribed by the rubrics or the S.R.C. The latter has ruled that it may be made of cotton, wool, or hemp;[119] however, brocade, silk poplin or damask are the preferred materials.[120] Although the draped veil may be tight-fitting, the preferred style seems to demand that it be made of such material and in such form as will permit it to drape gracefully over the tabernacle.[121]

Anson's description may well serve as a practical guide for the making of tabernacle veils:

> The most simple form consists of a single piece of material with a hem on top, through which a ribbon or tape is passed. This is tied up, allowing enough room to slip the veil over the small cross or emblem on the top. If the small cross or emblem is removable, the *conopeum* may be neatly fitted and kept in position.
>
> Normally the veil is open all the way in front, unless it is thought better to sew the top part. But if not sewn it is easier to turn back the veil and open the tabernacle door.[122]

116 *Churches,* p. 94.

117 *The Book of Ceremonies,* p. 6.

118 *The Church Edifice,* p. 99; cf. also Lallou and Talbot, "The Textile Appurtenances of the Altar," *Liturgical Arts* (New York, 1931—) I (1931-32), 56.

119 S.R.C., *Briocen.,* 21 iul. 1855, ad 10—*Decr. Auth.,* n. 3035.

120 Anson, *Churches,* p. 94.

121 Anson, *Churches,* p. 94; Collins, *The Church Edifice,* p. 99; L. O'Connell, *The Book of Ceremonies,* p. 6.

122 *Churches,* pp. 94-95.

3. Color

The color of the tabernacle veil may be white; however, it seems to be more in accord with the practice of the Church in Rome that the color of the veil correspond to the rubrical color of the day.[123] At Requiem Masses, however, the color of the veil is to be not black but violet.[124] For exposition of the Blessed Sacrament, the veil should be white.[125] However, if exposition immediately follows Mass, then for the veil there may be retained the color of the office of the day, provided always that the black color be excluded.[126]

Article III: Altar Cloths and Frontals.

A. *Altar Cloths*

> *Hoc altare operiatur tribus mappis seu tobaleis mundis, ab Episcopo vel alio habente potestatem benedictis, superiori saltem oblonga, quae usque ad terram pertingat, duabus aliis brevioribus, vel una duplicata.*[127]
>
> *Tum in superna linea mappae mundae tres saltem explicentur, quae totam Altaris planitiem et latera contegant.*[128]

The directions of the *Missal* and the *Ceremonial* order that the altar on which Mass is celebrated be covered with three cloths. This seems to be one rubric that is universally known and observed. The top cloth is not only to cover the entire top of the *mensa,* but also should reach to the ground on the two end sides of the altar; the ends of this cloth should not touch the floor. The practice of using cloths which are so short that they do not extend to the ground in this manner has been condemned.[129] This upper cloth does not have to extend over the front edge of the altar, as seems to be the common practice in the United States. Liturgical writers bewail this custom and state that it is better to have this cloth lie

[123] S.R.C., *Briocen.*, 21 iul. 1885, ad 10, *Decr. Auth.*, n. 3035.

[124] S.R.C., *Nesqualien.*, 1 dec. 1882—*Decr. Auth.*, n. 3562.

[125] S.R.C., *Taggen.*, 9 iul. 1678, ad 7, 8, 9—*Decr. Auth.*, n. 1615; *Hispalen.*, 19 dec. 1829—*Decr. Auth.*, n. 2673.

[126] S.R.C., *Annecien.*, 1 dec. 1882—*Decr. Auth.*, n. 3559.

[127] *Missale Romanum,* Tit. *Rubricae Generales Missae,* Cap. XX.

[128] *Caeremoniale Episcoporum,* Lib. I, Cap. XII, n. 11.

[129] S.R.C., *Resolutionis Dubiorum,* 9 iun. 1899, ad I—*Decr. Auth.*, n. 4029.

along the edge of the *mensa.*[130] Anson gives sound reasons: first, from a practical point of view, if this cloth hangs over the edge, it is easily rubbed and thereby becomes soiled and crumpled; second, in the Roman basilicas the altar cloth does not hang over the front edge but runs flush with the top of the *mensa.*[131] .

Although the *Ceremonial* seems to imply that the two lower cloths should also extend over the sides of the altar,[132] the *Missal* states that they are shorter than the top cloth and that they may consist of one cloth folded double. These cloths should cover the entire surface of the *mensa* in length and width, even though the altar be only a portable altar.[133] J. O'Connell states that if the altar is a portable altar, at least the altar stone itself should be totally covered with these cloths.[134]

The proper material for the altar cloths is linen or hemp. The *Missal,* it is true, does not specify the material; the *Ceremonial,* however, says that the altar is to be covered with linen cloths.[135] A General Decree of the S.R.C. prescribes linen or hemp as the proper material for the altar cloths, and specifically proscribes the use of cotton.[136] The use of other materials has likewise been condemned, although the S.R.C. has permitted that cloths made of forbidden materials be used until they are worn out.[137]

The S.R.C. has granted two exceptions to the rule that linen alone is to be used, but only in particular cases. The first was granted in favor of a Vicariate-Apostolic in China, where unusual circumstances made it practically impossible to obtain linen. The material permitted in this case was *Ho-ma,* or grass cloth, which is similar in origin and structure to linen or hemp.[138] The second permission was granted to the Bishop of Vicenza. The S.R.C. al-

130 Anson, *Churches,* p. 117; L. O'Connell, *The Book of Ceremonies,* p. 20.
131 *Churches,* p. 118.
132 *Loc. cit.*
133 Anson, *Churches,* p. 117; L. O'Connell, *The Book of Ceremonies,* p. 20.
134 *The Celebration of Mass,* I, 245.
135 *Loc. cit.*
136 *Decretum Generale,* 15 maii 1819—*Decr. Auth.,* n. 2600.
137 *Placentina in Hispania,* 13 aug. 1895—*Decr. Auth.,* n. 3868.
138 *Vicariatus Apostolici Se-Ciuensis Sept.—Occidentalis,* 27 iun. 1898—*Decr. Auth.,* n. 3995.

lowed that, for his diocese, all the furnishings which ordinarily are made of linen, except the corporals, palls, and purificators, could be made of *rami*.[139]

Although the S.R.C. has stated that the altar cloths may be ornamented at the edges, i. e. at the front and the side, with laces which contain representations of crosses, monstrances, chalices, hosts, figures of angels, and other similar objects,[140] the commentaries consider the practice inartistic and impractical.[141] Anson suggests the use of embroidery in preference to lace, provided "the patterns are not too obtrusive."[142]

In addition to the three cloths required by the rubrics, the *Pontifical*[143] requires another, the cere-cloth which is termed *chrismale;* this is a waxed linen cloth. This is absolutely required only for the consecration of a fixed altar. It does not have to remain on the altar permanently, but should remain there as long as any traces of the Holy Oils remain on the *mensa*. Its position is beneath the three altar cloths, directly on the *mensa*. In Rome, the cere-cloth is always kept on the altar.[144] This cloth appears to be a very practical permanent furnishing, even for portable altars, in view of the fact that it protects the altar cloths from dampness.[145]

Another cloth, the altar cover or *vesperale* as it is called, though not prescribed by the rubrics, is highly recommended by the authors.[146] This is a purely utilitarian furnishing; it is in reality a dust cover, and seems to be almost essential or at least very helpful in preventing the altar cloths from becoming stained or

139 *De usu "rami,"—Coll. Decr.*, n. 82.

140 S.R.C., *Suren.*, 5 dec. 1868, ad V—*Decr. Auth.*, n. 3191; *Meliten.*, 20 mart. 1869, ad 5—*Decr. Auth.*, n. 3195.

141 Anson, *Churches*, p. 117; J. O'Connell, *The Celebration of Mass*, I, 245.

142 *Churches*, p. 117.

143 Tit. *De Consecratione Altaris.*

144 Anson, *Churches*, p. 118.

145 Wapelhorst, *Compendium Sacrae Liturgiae*, n. 18; L. O'Connell, *The Book of Ceremonies*, p. 21.

146 Anson, *Churches*, p. 121; Wapelhorst, *Compendium Sacrae Liturgiae*, n. 18; L. O'Connell, *The Book of Ceremonies*, p. 21; Collins, *The Church Edifice*, p. 161.

soiled. It must of course be removed from the altar during Mass.[147] No particular material is prescribed for this cloth, but it seems that it should be made of linen, silk, or some other rich material.[148] It may be of any color except black.[149] Red or green, however, appear to be the preferred colors,[150] with green being considered the "correct" color for ordinary occasions. Violet is considered the appropriate color for penitential seasons.[151]

Very frequently the *vesperale* is decorated in various ways; however, inasmuch as it is not a liturgical furnishing, it seems preferable that it be as simple and as inconspicuous as possible.[152]

B. *Frontals*

> *Pallio quoque [altare] ornetur coloris, quoad fieri potest, diei Festo vel Officio convenientis.*[153]
>
> *Paramenta Altaris . . . debent esse coloris convenientis Officio et Missae diei, secundum usum Romanae Ecclesiae: quae quinque coloribus uti consuevit. Albo, Rubeo, Viridi, Violaceo et Nigro.*[154]
>
> *Ipsum vero altare majus in festivitatibus solemnioribus, aut Episcopo celebraturo, quo splendidius poterit, pro temporum tamen varietate et exigentia, ornabitur: quod si a pariete disjunctum et separatum sit, apponentur, tam a parte anteriori, quam posteriori illius, pallia aurea, vel argentea, aut serica, auro perpulchre contexta, coloris festivitati congruentis, eaque sectis quadratisque lignis munita, quae telaria vocant, ne rugosa, aut sinuosa sed extensa, et explicata decentius conspiciantur.*[155]

The altar frontal is a cloth or tapestry which covers the entire front of the altar from the *mensa* to the platform. It is the "true liturgical decoration of the altar."[156] It is clearly prescribed by

147 S.R.C., *Cuneen.*, 2 iun. 1883, ad II—*Decr. Auth.*, n. 3576.
148 Anson, *Churches*, p. 121; L. O'Connell, *The Book of Ceremonies*, p. 21.
149 L. O'Connell, *op. cit.*, *loc cit.*
150 Collins, *The Church Edifice*, p. 162.
151 Anson, *Churches*, p. 121.
152 *Loc. cit.*
153 *Missale Romanum*, Tit. *Rubricae Generales Missalis*, Cap. XX.
154 *Ibid.*, Cap. XVIII.
155 *Caeremoniale Episcoporum*, Lib. I, Cap. XII, n. 11.
156 Collins, *The Church Edifice*, p. 136.

the *Missal,*[157] and the *Ceremonial* appears to require it at least for the greater feasts.[158] There are no decrees of the S.R.C. which require the use of the frontal, although one forbids the use of an abbreviated frontal, i.e., one that covers only a part of the front of the altar.[159] Some writers are most insistent that the frontal is of strict obligation. "Liturgical tradition and the rubrics demand the use of the frontal."[160] "It is difficult to understand why so many priests who are most punctilious about veiling tabernacles . . . ignore the rubrics concerning the proper clothing of the altar."[161]

Most authors, however, seem to be agreed that if the actual front of the altar is ornamented with metal or wood, or made in the style of a sepulchre, no frontal is required except on great feasts.[162]

In the United States the use of the frontal has practically fallen into desuetude in most places. Its continued use at funeral services constitutes a potential exception. Anson notes that the use of frontals disappeared in most places from the time of the Renaissance period. He notes, too, that it is difficult to understand that this practice of not using the frontal should have begun at the time it did. For sixteen centuries the frontal had been used almost universally; and then, just at the time when the rubrics specifically commanded the use of it, the frontal began to disappear from use.

At any rate, it appears that this rubric is almost universally disregarded today, at least in the United States and England. Cappello holds that, at least in so far as a marble altar is concerned, or one which is sufficiently decorated, the non-use of the frontal cannot be considered sinful; it has become custom which is valid in many dioceses for the very reason that the Holy See has re-

157 *Loc. cit.*

158 *Loc. cit.*

159 S.R.C., *Mexicana,* 10 sept. 1898, ad 2—*Decr. Auth.,* n. 4000.

160 J. O'Connell, *The Celebration of Mass,* I, 245.

161 Anson, *Churches,* p. 119.

162 Cappello, *De Sacramentis,* I, n. 725; L. O'Connell, *The Book of Ceremonies,* p. 7; Wapelhorst, *Compendium Sacrae Liturgiae,* n. 20; Collins, *The Church Edifice,* p. 137.

mained silent on the matter.[163] From the statements of Anson it appears that the frontal has not been used in most places for a period of some three hundred years; this, coupled with the fact that the Holy See has remained silent, that is, has not condemned the practice of its non-use, gives one a valid reason for concluding that a contrary custom has been established, and that the use of frontals is no longer obligatory in those places where it has not been used for such a long period.

The authors, however, usually consider the non-use of the frontal to be legitimate only if the front of the altar is properly decorated. So it seems that, if an altar is very simple in design, the frontal must be used.[164] Collins takes a middle position in stating that it is certainly the mind of the Church that the frontal be used on the main altar at least on the more solemn feasts and even on every Sunday of the year.[165]

No particular material is prescribed as proper for the frontal. Hence, any suitable fabric may be used, though it seems that a more precious material should be employed, preferably silk; in color at least it should conform to the color of the vestments of the particular church. The rubrics prescribe that the proper color of the frontal is the color of the feast of the day.[166] These are white, green, red, violet, and black. The *Ceremonial* permits, in fact recommends, the use of silver or gold frontals for great feasts.

Exceptions to this rule of color are the following: when the Blessed Sacrament is exposed, the frontal must be white.[167] However, if Exposition follows immediately after Mass or Vespers, the frontal which corresponds to the color of the office of the day or of the Mass, with the exception always of black, may be retained.[168]

163 *De Sacramentis,* I, n. 725.

164 Cf. *supra.,* p. 107.

165 *The Church Edifice,* p. 137.

166 *Missale Romanum, loc. cit.; Caeremoniale Episcoporum, loc. cit.*

167 S.R.C., *Taggen.,* 9 iul. 1678, ad 7—*Decr. Auth.,* n. 1615; *Hispalen.,* 19 dec. 1829—*Decr. Auth.,* n. 2673.

168 *Annecien.,* 1 dec. 1882—*Decr. Auth.,* n. 3559.

A black frontal is not to be used on the altar where the Blessed Sacrament is reserved. On such altars, the S.R.C. orders that violet frontals be used in place of black ones.[169]

The S.R.C. has issued no decrees regarding the ornamentation of the frontal except to forbid the use of the skull and cross bones.[170] Inasmuch as the S.R.C. has forbidden the depicting of the Sacred Heart separated from His Body as well as similar ones of the Immaculate Heart of Mary for use on the altar, it appears that such emblems should not appear on frontals.[171]

Article IV: Other Altar Furnishings: Altar Cards, Missal Stand, *Sanctus* Bell, Cruets, Communion Cloth, Communion Plate

> *In cornu Epistolae cussinus supponendus Missali: et ab eadem parte Epistolae paretur cereus ad elevationem Sacramenti accendendus, parva campanula, ampullae vitreae vini et aquae cum pelvicula et manutergio mundo, in fenestella seu in parva mensa ad haec praeparata.*[172]
>
> *Libri vero Missalis, Evangeliorum, Epistolarum, tecti serico eiusdem coloris quo cetera paramenta, cum pulvino ex eodem serico et colore, vel parvo legili argenteo, aut ligneo affabre tamen elaborato, ponuntur super credentia in cornu Epistolae.*[173]

A. *Altar Cards*

Before the sixteenth century there was apparently no regulation regarding the use of altar cards.[174] The first prescription ordering the use of an altar card appeared in the rubrics of the *Missal* published by St. Pius V in 1570. Since that time it appears to

169 *Montis Regalis,* 20 mart. 1869, ad 10—*Decr. Auth.,* n. 3201; *Nesqualien.,* 1 dec. 1882—*Decr. Auth.,* n. 3562. Collins notes that some authors maintain that a black frontal may be used for a funeral Mass or a Requiem on an altar where the Blessed Sacrament is reserved, provided that the altar is the only or the principal altar (*op. cit.* p. 142). Such an opinion seems to be contrary to the decrees of the S.R.C.

170 *Dubiorum,* 24 nov. 1905—*Decr., Auth.,* n. 4174.

171 S.R.C., *Marianopolitana.,* 5 apr. 1879—*Decr. Auth.,* n. 3492.

172 *Missale Romanum,* Tit. *Rubricae Generales Missalis,* Cap. XX.

173 *Caeremoniale Episcoporum,* Lib. I, Cap. XII, n. 15.

174 Anson, *Churches,* p. 128; Cappello, *De Sacramentis,* I, n. 729.

have become an almost indispensable accessory for the celebration of Mass; however, even today, altar cards are not used by bishops and certain other prelates for Pontifical Masses; these prelates read the prayers from the book known as the *Canon Missae.*

Actually, the present day practice of using three cards is not in accord with the rubrics. The *Missal* mentions only one card. The authors, however, aver that the custom is legitimate.[175] Anson and Cappello note at the same time that the card containing the first part of the Gospel of St. John, which is placed on the Gospel side of the altar, was introduced in the seventeenth century; later, very likely only for the sake of symmetry, the third card, which is placed on the Epistle side of the altar and which contains the prayers said by the celebrant when blessing the water and when washing his hands, was introduced.[176] The authors appear to be very safe in asserting that the use of three cards is now a laudably established custom in view of the fact that the S.R.C. has given at least an indirect confirmation of the practice in one of its decrees, which orders that the three altar cards are to be removed for the Exposition of the Blessed Sacrament.[177]

There are in the rubrics or in the decrees of the S.R.C. no provisions regarding the material, size or shape of the cards. However, a few points of design can be deduced from the fact that the cards are purely utilitarian in nature. They contain certain texts from the Ordinary of the Mass; although these prayers are also in the *Missal,* it is far more convenient for the celebrant to read them from the cards. The prayers which are usually on the cards are: the *Gloria* and *Credo;* the prayers before the Gospel, *Munda cor meum* and *Dominus sit;* the offertory prayers: *Suscipe, sancte Pater; Deus, qui humanae substantiae; Offerimus tibi; In spiritu; Veni, sanctificator; Lavabo;* and *Suscipe, sancta Trinitas;* the prayers at the Consecration, *Qui pridie, Hoc est, Simili modo, Hic est,* and *Haec quotiescumque;* the prayers before Communion,

175 Anson, *Churches,* p. 128; Cappello, *De Sacramentis,* I, n. 729; Collins, *The Church Edifice,* p. 159; J. O'Connell, *The Celebration of Mass,* I, 250; L. O'Connell, *The Book of Ceremonies,* p. 17.

176 Anson, *Churches,* p. 128; Cappello, *De Sacramentis,* I, n. 729.

177 *Tertii Ordinis S. Francisci,* 20 dec. 1864, ad 3—*Decr. Auth.,* n. 3130.

Domine Jesu Christe, qui, Domine Jesu Christe, Fili, Perceptio Corporis; prayer before the last blessing, *Placeat;* the Last Gospel, *In principio.*

Some of the more recently published cards also contain the prayers which the priest says immediately after the prayers at the foot of the altar, namely, *Aufer a nobis* and *Oramus;* some, too, have the prayers for the incensation after the Offertory: *Per intercessionem; Incensum istud; Dirigatur, Domine.* The newer cards, too, often omit the prayers before Communion. One should recall, however, that many of the prayers indicated above are to be said from memory according to the rubrics. The altar card could be said to contain such prayers only for the convenience of the celebrant if he should, as happens on occasion, suffer a short lapse of memory.

Inasmuch as the cards are supposed to be a help to the celebrant, it is in accord with good sense that the prayers be arranged in so far as possible in such a manner as not to force the celebrant to have to peer around the chalice to read them.[178]

Since the purpose of the cards is purely utilitarian, ornamentation and illumination seem to be entirely out of place on these cards; such additions are a hindrance rather than a help. The designer or printer of the cards should bear in mind their purpose "to put before the eyes of the celebrant, so arranged as to be easily found, so printed as to be read without difficulty, certain texts from the Ordinary of the Mass."[179] Hence, the most important consideration should be that the cards be printed in large, bold, clear, legible type. If ornamentation is used, it should be utilized in such a way as to help the celebrant locate the prayers. A frame with a narrow, simple moulding is the most suitable. In order to keep the cards clean, it is best that they be framed under glass or covered with mica;[180] this latter type of card has enjoyed great popularity in recent years.

When the cards are not being used, i.e. after Mass, it seems

[178] Collins, *The Church Edifice,* p. 160.
[179] J. O'Connell, *The Celebration of Mass,* I, 250.
[180] *Loc. cit.*

best to remove them from the altar.[181] Cappello, however, notes, that this practice is nowhere actually prescribed by the rubrics, and that the writers are in error in teaching that the cards must be removed; he sees no objection to the practice of turning the cards down on the altar and covering them with the *vesperale*.[182]

The only regulation of the S.R.C. regarding the altar cards has already been noted, namely that they are to be removed for Exposition of the Blessed Sacrament except during the time of Mass.[183]

B. *The Missal Cushion or Stand*

The rubrics of the *Missal*[184] further add that a cushion is to be placed on the altar to support the *Missal.* The *Ceremonial*[185] also orders the use of such a cushion, but also allows a small stand to be used in its place. If the cushion or pillow is used, it should be covered with silk of a color that corresponds to the color of the office of the day or of the Mass.

Today, in the United States at least, the stand appears to be the instrument which, to the writer's knowledge, is used most commonly, if not also universally. In many places it is customary to cover the stand with a piece of silk conforming in material and color to that of the vestments. This practice seems to be very praiseworthy and in accord with the spirit of the rubric which requires such ornamentation for the *Missal* cushion. No covering should be used at Requiem Masses.[186]

The liturgical books and the decrees of the S.R.C. do not contain any directions concerning the construction of the *Missal* stand. The *Ceremonial* states however that it should be made of

181 Anson, *Churches,* p. 129; Collins, *The Church Edifice,* p. 160; J. O'Connell, *The Celebration of Mass,* I, 250; L. O'Connell, *The Book of Ceremonies,* p. 17; Cappello, *De Sacramentis,* I, n. 729.

182 *Loc. cit.*

183 Cf. *supra,* p. 111.

184 *Loc. cit.*

185 *Loc. cit.*

186 Anson, *Churches,* p. 129; J. O'Connell, *The Celebration of Mass,* I, 251; L. O'Connell, *The Book of Ceremonies,* p. 17.

silver, or of wood artistically *(affabre)* decorated.[187] The type of stand which is recommended is "a light stand, inconspicuous, stoutly made, well balanced, which takes up small space and is sufficiently high."[188] Anson[189] and J. O'Connell[190] go into great detail in recommending a type of stand which is less widely used in the United States. This is a stand which rests on a pillar with a round broad base. Such a stand has several advantages over the type ordinarily used, i.e. over the kind that has legs. The latter type has the following disadvantages: its structure makes it difficult for the celebrant to place his hands just outside the corporal; it is more difficult for the *Missal* to be drawn sufficiently near to be read; the left front leg has a tendency to fall off the *mensa,* and the right front leg to intrude itself onto the corporal.[191]

C. *The Credence and the Cruets*

> 19. *Restat, ut de mensa, seu abaca, quam credentiam vocant, pauca subjiciamus. Ea vero in Missis tantum solemnioribus praeparari solet a latere Epistolae in plano Presbyterii, si loci dispositio patiatur, atque a pariete parumper disjuncta; ita ut inter illam et parietem stare possint familiares Episcopi, ad manuum lotionem destinati, nisi propter loci angustiam id fieri non possit . . . ; quo casu fiet, prout melius poterit. Ejus mensura regulariter erit palmorum octo in longitudine, in latitudine quatuor vel circa, in altitudine quinque, vel modicum ultra; lineoque mantili mundo superstrato, usque ad terram circumcirca pendenti, contergetur.*[192]

1. The Cruets

The rubric of the *Missal* directs that the cruets for wine and water be made of glass or clear crystal.[193] The reason for this direction is most probably to be sought in the existing danger of confusing the wine cruet with the water cruet; furthermore, it

[187] *Loc. cit.*

[188] L. O'Connell, *The Book of Ceremonies,* p. 17.

[189] *Churches,* p. 129.

[190] *The Celebration of Mass,* I, 251.

[191] *Loc. cit.*

[192] *Caeremoniale Episcoporum,* Lib. I, Cap. XII, n. 19.

[193] *Loc. cit.*

becomes an easier task to keep them perfectly clean.[194] In earlier days the cruets were rarely made of glass or crystal, but usually of metal,[195] a practice which is still permitted.[196] When metal cruets are used, they should be clearly marked, so that the water cruet will be easily distinguishable from the wine cruet.

The cruets should be provided with loose-fitting stoppers which serve to exclude dust and insects, particularly from the wine. A small tray of metal or glass should be provided for the holding of the cruets. There should also be a small bowl or dish which receives the water used in the washing of the priest's fingers; also a small towel for the drying of the fingers.[197] This towel should be changed frequently.

2. The *Sanctus* Bell

One other furnishing is prescribed by the rubric of the *Missal* as one of the ordinary prerequisites for the celebration of Mass, namely the *sanctus* bell.[198] The word used in the rubric is *parva campanula;* this indicates that a small hand bell is to be used.[199] Actually, there are no prescriptions or regulations regarding the size or material of the bell. It is generally admitted that the correct bell is one done in silver or bronze with only one tongue. Chiming bells are not forbidden.[200] The S.R.C., however, has forbidden the use of a gong type bell, that is, a cymbal or a basinlike instrument attached to a shaft.[201]

3. The Credence Table

The cruets, their accessories, and the bell are to be placed on the credence table. This should be covered with a white cloth; on the more solemn feasts, at least, this cloth should extend all

194 J. O'Connell, *The Celebration of Mass,* I, 252.

195 Anson, *Churches,* p. 129.

196 S.R.C., *S. Iacobi de Cile,* 28 apr. 1866—*Decr. Auth.,* n. 3149.

197 J. O'Connell, *The Celebration of Mass,* I, 252; Anson, *Churches,* p. 130.

198 *Loc. cit.*

199 Cf. *Missale Romanum,* Tit. *Ritus Servandus in celebratione Missae,* Cap. VII, n. 6.

200 J. O'Connell, *The Celebration of Mass,* I, 252; L. O'Connell, *The Book of Ceremonies,* p. 18; Anson, *Churches,* p. 130.

201 *Mexicana,* 10 sept. 1898, ad 3—*Decr. Auth.,* n. 4000.

the way to the floor on all sides of the table.[202] On the less solemn feasts, it seems, this covering need not extend so far.[203] The rubrics of the *Missal* mention the use of a *"fenestella,"* a small window, or a niche, or a bracket on the wall for the credence table. Anson takes this to mean a smaller wicker basket in which the cruets and their accessories are carried, as is the custom in the city of Rome.[204]

D. *The Communion Cloth and Communion Paten*

> *Interim minister ante eos (qui sunt communicandi) extendit linteum seu velum album.*[205]
>
> *. . . eodemque tempore vocentur duo Capellani, seu acolythi, cottis induti cum mantili albo, quod genuflexi sustinent ante communicandos, hinc inde ambabus manibus per quatuor angulos, quousque perfecta fuerit communio.*[206]
>
> *Interim minister ante eos extendit lintem seu velum album.*[207]
>
> 5. In distributing Holy Communion to the faithful, in addition to the white linen cloth spread before the communicants, according to the Rubrics of the *Missal,* the *Ritual,* and the *Bishops' Ceremonial,* a paten should be used, which should be of silver or gilded metal, but not engraved on the inside, and which should be held by the faithful themselves under their chins, except in the case where Holy Communion is given by a Bishop, or by a prelate in pontificals, or in a solemn Mass, when a priest or deacon who is in attendance may hold the paten under the chins of the communicants.
>
> 7. . . . It is not, however, the mind of the Sacred Congregation to condemn the patens, of whatever form they may be, which are now used in certain churches, pro-

---

202 *Caeremoniale Episcoporum, loc. cit.*

203 L. O'Connell, *The Book of Ceremonies,* p. 18.

204 Anson, *Churches,* p. 130.

205 *Missale Romanum,* Tit. *Ritus Servandus in celebratione Missae,* Cap. X, n. 6.

206 *Caeremoniale Episcoporum,* Lib. II, Cap. XXIX, n. 3.

207 *Rituale Romanum,* Tit. IV, Cap. II, n. 12.

vided they be made of metal, not engraved on the inside, and be suitable to catch the sacred fragments.[208]

These excerpts from the *Rubrics* of the liturgical books make it very clear that a communion cloth is to be spread before those who are about to receive Holy Communion. The use of the paten was ordered by the Congregation of the Sacraments as a measure of added precaution. Because of this instruction, some authors have presumed that the communion cloth need be used no longer.[209] However, the very wording of the Instruction, "in addition to the white linen cloth," appears to make such an interpretation improper and incorrect. At any rate, the practice of using only the paten and of disregarding the rubrics regarding the communion cloth seems to have gained very widespread acceptance in the United States, although there appears to be no basis for it in the law.

The practice is supported, perhaps, in view of a decree of the S.R.C., *Romana,* 16 mart. 1876, in which the Congregation did not condemn the practice of using a paten in place of the communion cloth. Although this decree is cited by the Congregation of the Sacraments as the basis for the widespread use of the paten, it should be noted that the decree does not appear in the *Decreta Authentica* of the S.R.C.

The wording of the *Instruction* of the Congregation of the Sacraments in directing that the communicant himself hold the paten while he is receiving seems to make the use of the communion cloth impractical, except, as Collins notes, that it is to rest on the top of the communion rail.[210]

Prior to the introduction of the paten, the practice seems to have been that the communicant held the communion cloth under his chin.[211]

A very practical solution which some churches follow, is to

[208] S.C. de Sacramentis *Instructio,* 26 mart. 1929, *Adnotationes,* n. 5 et n. 7—*AAS,* XXI (1929), 638. (Translation from Bouscaren, *The Canon Law Digest,* I, 362.)

[209] Cf. Anson, *Churches,* p. 122.

[210] *The Church Edifice,* p. 221.

[211] Gasparri, *De SS. Eucharistia,* n. 1182.

have the communicant hold the communion cloth under his chin, while an altar boy holds the paten. This is not forbidden by the *Instruction*[212] and it certainly serves to achieve more efficiently the object of the prescription, namely, the use of a safeguard that will prevent particles from falling to the ground.

The liturgical books and the decrees of the S.R.C. do not prescribe the dimensions or the form of the communion cloth. However, it is recommended that the cloth be attached to the communion rail and that it be of the same depth as the communion rail. The most suitable material, though not strictly prescribed by the rubrics, seems to be linen.[213]

The material of the paten is prescribed by the *Instruction.*[214] It is to be made of silver or of some other metal which must be gilded, but is not to be engraved on the inside.

E. *Other Altar Decorations, namely, reliquaries, statues, flowers*

> *Super Altare nihil omnino ponatur, quod ad Missae sacrificium vel ipsius altaris ornatum non pertineat.*[215]
>
> *Si vero in Altari fuerint Reliquiae, seu Imagines Sanctorum, incensata Cruce, et facta ei reverentia, antequam discedat a medio altaris, primum incensat eas quae a dexteris sunt, idest a parte Evangelii prope crucem, bis ducens thuribulum, et iterum facta Cruci reverentia, similiter incensat bis alias, quae sunt a sinistris, hoc est a parte Epistolae . . .* [216]
>
> *Celebrante vero Episcopo, candelabra septem super altari ponantur, quo casu crux non in medio illorum, sed ante altius candelabrum in medio cereorum positum locabitur, a cujus lateribus, si haberentur aliquae Reliquiae, aut tabernacula cum Sanctorum Reliquiis vel imagines argenteae exponi possent; quae quidem sacrae Reliquiae et imagines, cum sex tantum candelabra super altari erunt,*

---

212 Cf. S.C. Sacr., Reply to the Bishop of Rodez, 19 sept., 1930 in Bouscaren, *The Canon Law Digest,* II, 193-194.

213 Collins, *The Church Edifice,* p. 221.

214 *Loc. cit.*

215 *Missale Romanum,* Tit. *Rubricae Generales Missalis,* Cap. XX.

216 *Missale Romanum,* Tit. *Ritus Servandus in celebratione Missae,* Cap. IV, n. 5.

disponi poterunt alternatim inter ipsa candelabra: dummodo ipsa altaris dispositio et longitudo id patiatur; sed et vascula cum flosculis, frondibusque odoriferis, seu serico contextis, studiose ornata adhiberi poterunt.[217]

Although the General Rubrics of the *Missal* order that absolutely nothing be placed on the altar if it does not pertain to the sacrifice of the Mass or to the actual ornamentation of the altar, in the *Ritus Servandus* the rubrics allude to the potential presence of reliquaries and statues on the altar. In like manner the diagram for incensing the altar, given in the Missal just before the *Proprium de Tempore,* indicates that reliquaries or statues may be placed on the altar. This is further borne out by the *Ceremonial,* which also admits of the use of flowers, real or artificial, especially on the greater feast days.

Reliquaries and statues are properly placed between the candlesticks. They are not to be placed on the tabernacle where the Blessed Sacrament is reserved.[218] Neither are they to be placed before the door of the tabernacle,[219] nor on the throne which is used for the Exposition of the Blessed Sacrament.[220]

Although the *Ceremonial* seems to recommend the use of flowers for the greater feast days, liturgical writers are of the opinion that they should be used only "with the greatest restraint."[221] However, as Collins notes, "the use of flowers to decorate the altar . . . is in entire accord with the traditional usages of the Church. . . . Not to allow any flowers on the altar for the sake of being 'liturgical' is another example of misplaced zeal."[222]

The proper position for flowers appears to be the space that obtains between the candlesticks.[223] They are not to be placed

217 *Caeremoniale Episcoporum,* Lib. I, Cap. XII, n. 12.

218 S.R.C., *Decretum Generale,* 4 apr. 1821, ad 6—*Decr. Auth.,* n. 2613.

219 S.R.C., *Sancti Angeli in Vado,* 6 sept. 1845—*Decr. Auth.,* n. 2906.

220 S.R.C., *Goana,* 19 sept. 1883—*Decr. Auth.,* n. 3589.

221 J. O'Connell, *The Celebration of Mass,* I, 246; cf. also Anson, *Churches,* p. 125.

222 *The Church Edifice,* p. 154.

223 Collins, *op. cit.,* p. 156; J. O'Connell, *op. cit., loc. cit.*

before the door of the tabernacle;[224] *a fortiori,* the places in which it is forbidden to set statues and reliquaries seem also to exclude the placing of flowers, namely, the tabernacle and the throne used for Exposition.

224 S.R.C., *Congregationis Montis Coronae,* 22 ian. 1701, ad 10—*Decr. Auth.,* n. 2067.

CHAPTER X

THE SACRED VESSELS AND THEIR APPURTENANCES

Article I: The Sacred Vessels

A. *Chalices and Paten*

> . . . *Deinde praeparat Calicem (qui debet esse vel aureus vel argenteus, aut saltem habere cuppam argenteam intus inauratam, et simul cum Patena itide minaurata, ab Episcopo consecratus), . . .*[1]
>
> . . . *si non adsit Calix cum Patena conveniens, cujus cuppa debet esse aurea vel argentea vel stannea, non aerea vel vitrea; . . .*[2]
>
> *Deinde in cornu Epistolae accipit Calicem, Purificatorio extergit, et sinistra tenens illius nodum, . . .*[3]

The most important of the sacred vessels is the chalice. According to the present legislation, as indicated in the rubrics quoted above, the chalice must be made of gold or silver, or must at least have a silver cup which is gold plated on the inside. This was reaffirmed by the S.R.C.[4] Hence, chalices made of any other material, e.g. wood, brass, copper, glass, may not be used, at least not in virtue of what is termed the ordinary law.[5] However, by extraordinary law, the basis of which is the rubric contained under the Title *Ritus Servandus,* a chalice whose cup is made of gold, silver, or tin, is admissible. By "extraordinary law" in this case is meant extreme poverty or some other necessity. When such causes are present, it appears that no permission is required

[1] *Missale Romanum,* Tit. *Ritus Servandus in Celebratione Missae,* Cap. I, n. 1.

[2] *Missale Romanum,* Tit. *De Defectibus in Celebratione Missarum Occurrentibus,* Cap. X, n. 1.

[3] *Missale Romanum,* Tit. *Ritus Servandus in Celebratione Missae,* Cap. VII, n. 4.

[4] *Aesina,* 16 sept. 1865 ad 4—*Decr. Auth.,* n. 3136.

[5] Cf. Cappello, *De Sacramentis,* I, n. 747.

before one may use a chalice made of tin.[6] In fact, the Constitution *Imposito Nobis* of Pope Benedict XIV[7] stated that there did not exist any general decree forbidding the use of a tin chalice if others are not available.

The paten is usually made of the same material as the cup of the chalice, but in view of the distinction made by the rubrics the authors are of the opinion that this is not necessary; however, it should be made of solid and becoming material and its upper surface must be gold plated.[8]

The rubrics prescribe nothing about the form of the chalice and paten. However, it can be deduced that the chalice is made up of three parts: the cup, the base, and the stem with a node. The introduction of new forms of chalices is left to the local ordinary, who is cautioned to see to it that chalices do not diverge from the traditional forms, so that all danger of spilling the Sacred Species and all scandal to the faithful shall be forestalled.[9]

J. O'Connell gives what appears to be a most suitable description of a proper and practical chalice:

> These parts [i.e. the cup, the stem with its node, and the base] must be so fashioned and united that the chalice may, as fully as possible, fulfill its object, i.e., to hold in absolute safety the Precious Blood, and be conveniently usable for the ceremonies of the Mass. In general, the chalice must be well balanced, so that there is no danger of its turning over when on the altar, or when lifted up by the priest. This requires that it be not too light in weight; nor must it be too heavy, since it would then be unwieldy to handle or raise. It must not be too high, or it will not be convenient for the Celebrant to make the signs of the cross over it, or to incense it at high Mass; nor yet too low when it will lose in dignity, and the average-sized chalice veil will not suit it. The shape of the cup is of much importance—if it is too wide or too shallow, there is danger of spilling the contents when elevating it, or when drinking from it or emptying it, or

[6] Cappello, *op. cit., loc. cit.*

[7] 29 mart. 1751, §3—*Fontes,* n. 410.

[8] Cappello, *De Sacramentis,* I, n. 748. Collins, *The Church Edifice,* p. 196.

[9] *S.R.C., Dubium,* 30 iun. 1922—*Decr. Auth.,* n. 4371.

> even if it should be jerked by accident; if it is too narrow, it is difficult to make the signs of the cross within it at *per Ipsum,* etc.; if it is too deep it is impossible to dry it after its purification. There should be no ornamentation on the outside of the cup near the edge, over which the Precious Blood will pass. That the Celebrant at Mass may conveniently hold the chalice *"iuxta* (or *"circa"*) *nodum infra cuppam,"* as the rubrics require,— and this between the first and second fingers, after the consecration of the Host—the node should be separated from the cup by a part of the stem, and the node should be round and smooth. The base should be heavy enough and wide enough so that the chalice will not easily overturn, yet not so wide as to take up undue space on an altar stone that may be of limited dimensions. All ornaments that project should be avoided on the foot of the chalice. On the base should be clearly marked a cross, so that the Celebrant may know at what part of the lip of chalice he drank the Precious Blood, and receive the ablutions at the same point.[10]

The paten is traditionally round in form; in size it should be a little larger in circumference than the top of the cup of the chalice, so that it will extend over the edge of the latter. It should be concave in shape, or have a circle in relief, so that it will sit firmly on the chalice. The outer surface (i.e., the under surface) may be engraved or decorated, but its inner surface should be entirely plain except for a small cross at one point near the edge to mark the spot which has been kissed by the celebrant. The edges of the paten should be very thin, though not cutting, inasmuch as it is used to gather up particles from the corporal. Patens which have a depressed center, like a plate, may perhaps offer some inconvenience though some priests prefer them. For a most practical paten one may perhaps think of a plain disc, free of all engravings and decorations, with a raised ring attached to the lower side.[11]

[10] *The Celebration of Mass,* I, 253-254.

[11] Anson, *Churches;* p. 180; Collins, *The Church Edifice,* pp. 196-197; J. O'Connell, *The Celebration of Mass,* I, 255.

B. *Ciborium.*

> 5. *Curare porro debet, ut particulae consecratae, eo numero sufficienti, pro communicandis Canonicis et aliis satis esse possit, perpetuo conserventur in pyxide ex solida decentique materia, eaque munda, et suo operculo bene clausa, cooperta albo velo serico, et, quantum res feret, ornato in tabernaculo inamovibili in media parte altaris posito et clave obserato.*[12]
>
> 2. *Nam servatis omnibus, quae superius in capite de Missa solemni, Episcopo celebrante, explicata sunt usque ad Offertorium, eo dicto, portatur per Subdiaconum vas argenteum vel aureum cum multis particulis prout populi frequentia requiret, coopertum, quod Diaconus collocat ante crucem; . . .* [13]
>
> 3. *Praeparentur cum Hostia consecranda particulae in numero qui infirmorum et aliorum fidelium communioni de clero communicare volentibus, in vase aureo vel argenteo, saltem intus deaurato, quod collocetur cum calice super altari, prout supra dictum est.*[14]

The ciborium is a vessel which is used for holding or containing the Sacred Particles consecrated at Mass and reserved in the tabernacle. The shape of the ciborium is not determined by the rubrics; however, it is traditionally similar to the chalice, i.e., it has a cup, a stem with a node, and a base. The cup is usually larger than that of the chalice and differently shaped; its normal diameter is about four inches, although some are much smaller and others are as wide as seven inches.[15] Many ciboria have at the bottom of the cup a slight elevation which makes it easier to take up the last few particles.[16] According to the rubric of the *Ritual* cited above, the cup of the ciborium must be fitted with a cover; this should be close-fitting *(bene clausa)* to exclude dust and damp; at the same time it should not be binding, since if force has to be used to remove the cover there is a danger that the Sacred Hosts will be spilled. This cover is to be separate, i.e.,

[12] *Rituale Romanum,* Tit. IV, Cap. I, n. 5; canon 1270.

[13] *Caeremoniale Episcoporum,* Liber II, Cap. XXIX, n. 2.

[14] *Ibid.,* Cap. XXX, n. 3.

[15] Anson, *Churches,* p. 181.

[16] Collins, *The Church Edifice,* p. 198; J. O'Connell, *The Celebration of Mass,* I, 255.

it is not to be attached to the cup with a hinge.[17] Although it is not prescribed by the rubrics, the cover of the ciborium is usually surmounted by a small cross; this serves to keep the veil in position.[18]

What has been stated about the node of the chalice[19] may be restated about the node of the ciborium, namely that it should be round, smooth, and free from projecting points. The base of the ciborium should be somewhat weighted, so that the possibility of its overturning may become minimized.[20]

While the rubric of the *Ritual* as also the Code prescribes that the ciborium be made of solid and becoming material, neither they nor the S.R.C. specify what these materials should be. The cited rubrics of the *Ceremonial* speak only of gold, silver, or at least of a cup which is gold plated. Most authors are firm in demanding that the cup at least be gold plated on the inside.[21] The S.R.C. has expressly permitted the use of ciboria which are made of copper but whose cups are gold-plated on the inside.[22] Unbecoming materials are: glass (which has been explicitly forbidden),[23] steel, lead, wood, ivory, etc.[24]

The *Ritual* and the Code prescribe that the ciborium be covered with a white, ornamented, silk veil. This veil must cover the ciborium when it contains the Blessed Sacrament. When it does not contain the Blessed Sacrament, there is a divergence of opinion as to whether or not this veil should cover the ciborium. Some authors[25] argue that whenever it is in public view and not in use it is to be covered in the fashion the S.R.C. has prescribed for the monstrance.[26] Others are of the opinion that the veil is a

17 Collins, *The Church Edifice,* p. 199; J. O'Connell, op. cit., I, 255.

18 Collins, *The Church Edifice,* p. 199.

19 *Supra.,* p. 150.

20 Collins, *op. cit., loc. cit.*

21 Anson, *Churches,* p. 180; Collins, *The Church Edifice,* p. 198; J. O'Connell, *The Celebration of Mass,* I, 255.

22 *Sancti Hippolyti,* 31 aug. 1867 ad 6—*Decr. Auth,* n. 3162.

23 S.R.C., *Mindonien.* 30 ian. 1880—*Decr. Auth.,* n. 3511.

24 Cappello, *De Sacramentis,* I, n. 336; Collins, *op. cit.,* p. 198.

25 J. O'Connell, *op. cit.,* I, 256; cf. Collins, *op. cit.,* p. 200.

26 *Westmonasterien.,* 27 maii 1911, ad VII—Decr. Auth., n. 4268.

sign of the presence of the Blessed Sacrament, and hence the ciborium should not be veiled except when it contains the Blessed Sacrament.[27] The latter opinion appears to be the one which is most commonly followed in the United States.

Article II: The Sacred Linens: Corporal, Pall, Purificator

> *. . . super eius os ponit Purificatorium, et super illud Patenam cum Hostia integra, quam leviter extergit, si opus est, a fragmentis, et eam tegit parva Palla linea, tum Velo serico; super Velo ponit Bursam coloris paramentorum intus habentem Corporale plicatum, quod ex lino tantum esse debet, nec serico, vel auro in medio intextum, sed totum album . . .*[28]
>
> 1. *Possunt etiam defectus occurrere in ministerio ipso, si aliquid ex requisitis ad illud desit: ut, . . . si Corporalia non sint munda, quae debent esse ex lino, nec serico in medio ornata . . .*[29]

The corporal, pall, and purificator, are prescribed by the rubrics as necessary for the celebration of Mass. Neither the rubrics nor the Decrees of the S.R.C. contain any prescriptions regarding the form or the size of these linens. Writers generally advise that the corporal should be large enough to hold the chalice, paten, and host conveniently, i.e., about twenty inches square.[30]

The pall should be large enough to cover the paten, that is to say, usually about seven inches square. It must be rigid enough to support the chalice veil. To attain such rigidity, the common practice in the United States appears to be the inserting of a piece of cardboard between two pieces of linen which have been sewn together on three sides. Though Collins approves this practice,[31] other authors frown on it as undesirable. A more recommended

[27] Cf. Collins, *op. cit., loc. cit.*

[28] *Missale Romanum,* Tit. *Ritus Servandus in Celebratione Missae,* Cap. I, n. 1.

[29] *Ibid.,* Tit. *De Defectibus in Celebratione Missarum occurrentibus,* Cap. X, n. 1.

[30] Anson, *Churches,* p. 121; Collins, *The Church Edifice,* p. 213; J. O'Connell, *The Celebration of Mass,* I, 257.

[31] *Op. cit.,* p. 215.

pall is one which is made from three or four thicknesses of linen and well starched.[32]

The purificator usually measures about twelve by eighteen inches.

Only one material is prescribed and permitted for corporals, palls and purificators, namely, linen. This is the material strictly prescribed by the *Missal*[33] for the corporal and pall. The S.R.C. has specifically prescribed that corporals, palls, and purificators, be made only of linen to the exclusion of any other materials.[34] In like manner, on specific occasions this Congregation has forbidden the use of muslin,[35] of a material made of ramie *(ex urticis confecta)*,[36] and of a material called *"Nipis,"* (which is actually fabricated in the same way as linen),[37] for the making of the sacred linens.

The authors are agreed that the corporal in accord with the prescriptions of the rubrics should be wholly plain, i.e., it should contain no ornamentation at all.[38] Usually the corporal has a small cross of red thread in the center of the front part of it. Although this practice is not condemned as unlawful, writers frown on it as unprescribed and meaningless.[39] Likewise, it is generally admitted that the corporal may be surrounded with a narrow border of lace, but this ornamentation too is not recommended.[40]

The most desirable pall appears to be one of the type that is generally in use, namely, pure white, with no ornamentation. The S.R.C., however, has permitted the use of palls whose upper side is embroidered with suitable symbols, covered with silk, gold, or silver, provided that this upper cloth is not black and does not bear any representations of death, and that the lower side be made of linen and be easily detachable.[41]

32 Anson, *Churches,* p. 122; J. O'Connell, *The Celebration of Mass,* I, 257.

33 *Loc. cit.*

34 S.R.C., *Decretum Generale,* 15 maii 1819—*Decr. Auth.,* n. 2600.

35 S.R.C., *Pisauren.,* 15 martii 1664—*Decr. Auth.,* n. 1287.

36 *Asculana in Piceno,* 17 dec. 1875—*Decr. Auth.,* n. 3387.

37 S.R.C., *Placentina in Hispania,* 13 aug. 1895—*Decr. Auth.,* n. 3868.

38 Anson, *op. cit.,* p. 121; Collins, *op. cit.,* p. 213; J. O'Connell, *op. cit.,* I, 257; L. O'Connell, *Book of Ceremonies,* p. 19.

39 J. O'Connell, *op. cit., loc. cit.*

40 *Loc. cit.*

41 S.R.C., *Dubiorum Resolutio,* 17 iul. 1894 ad 4—*Decr. Auth.,* n. 3832; *Dubiorum,* 24 nov. 1905 ad 2—*Decr. Auth.,* n. 4174.

Purificators are usually plain, but a small cross of colored thread in their center is usually recommended in order that they may readily be distinguished from finger towels.[42]

Article III: The Chalice Veil and Burse

These two appurtenances of the chalice are usually considered in the treatment of the vestments. However, inasmuch as they are strictly appurtenances of the chalice, it seems that the proper place for their consideration is in relation to the sacred vessels.

The rubrics prescribe that the chalice is to be adorned with the veil and burse.[43] No mention is made regarding the form or the material of these articles except that the veil is to be made of silk and the burse is to be of the color of the vestments. However, the general practice today and the common opinion of the authors is that the veil and burse should conform in material and color to the material and color of the vestments which the celebrant wears at Mass.[44] The veil should be large enough to cover the entire front of the chalice.[45]

[42] Collins, *The Church Edifice,* p. 218; J. O'Connell, *op. cit.* I, 258.

[43] Cf. *supra.,* p. 125.

[44] Cappello, *De Sacramentis,* I, n. 760.

[45] S.R.C., *Urbinitaten.,* 12 ian. 1669—*Decr. Auth.,* n. 1379.

CHAPTER XI

THE SACERDOTAL VESTMENTS

In Officio Missae, Celebrans semper utitur Planeta super Albam.[1]

2. *Quibus ita dispositis, accedit ad paramenta, quae non debent esse lacera, aut scissa, sed integra, et decenter munda, ac pulchra . . .*

3. *Ac primum accipiens Amictum circa extremitates et chordulas, osculatur illud in medio, ubi est Crux, et ponit super caput, et mox declinat ad collum, et eo vestium collaria circumtegens, ducit chordulas sub brachiis, et circumducens per dorsum, ante pectus reducit, et ligat. Tum Alba induitur, caput submittens, deinde manicam dexteram brachio dextero, et sinistram sinistro imponens. Albam ipsam corpori adaptat, elevat ante, et a lateribus hinc inde, et Cingulo, per ministrum a tergo sibi porrecto, se cingit. Minister elevat Albam super Cingulum circumcira, ut honeste dependeat, et tegat vestes; ac ejus fimbrias diligenter aptat, ut ad latitudinem digiti, vel circiter, super terram aequaliter fluat. Sacerdos accipit Manipulum, osculatur Crucem in medio, et imponit brachio sinistro. Deinde ambabus manibus accipiens Stolam, simili modo deosculatur, et imponit medium ejus collo, ac transversando eam ante pectus in modum crucis, ducit partem a sinistro humero pendentem, ad dexteram, et partem a dextero humero pendentem, ad sinistram. Sicque utramque partem Stolae extremitatibus Cinguli hinc inde ipsi Cingulo conjungit.*

4. . . . *Postremo Sacerdos accipit Planetuam.*[2]

It is plain that the Missal enumerates the following vestments as necessary for the celebration of Mass: amice, alb, cincture, maniple, stole, and chasuble. These are usually divided into two groups, the first group comprising the first three vestments enumerated, namely, the amice, alb, and cincture; these are commonly referred to as the inner vestments *(indumenta)*; the second group

[1] *Missale Romanum,* Tit. *Rubricae Generales Missalis,* Cap. XIX, n. 1.
[2] *Ibid.,* Tit. *Ritus Servandus in Celebratione Missae,* Cap. I, nn. 2-5.

comprises the maniple, stole, and chasuble, and are called the outer vestments *(paramenta)*.

It must be noted that the rubrics state no regulations regarding the form, size, material, or ornamentation of the vestments, except that they are to be beautiful. The Code, too, is silent about these matters, except that regarding the material and form it orders that one must follow the laws of the liturgy, the conventions of ecclesiastical tradition, and the canons of sacred art.[3] The chief official source for the proper form, material, and ornamentation of the sacred vestments is to be found in the Decrees of the S.R.C.

ARTICLE I: THE INNER VESTMENTS *(Indumenta)*: AMICE, ALB, CINCTURE

A. *Amice and Alb*

The amice is a square or rectangular piece of linen with two tapes sewn to its top corners. It is the first vestment which the priest puts on when vesting for Mass. It should be neatly hemmed all around.[4] The amice should be sufficiently large in view of the fact that it is to cover the back as well as the breast of the celebrant and is to be tucked in around the neck. The average recommended size is 24 by 36 inches.[5] The tapes or strings, too, should be sufficiently long; they are to be crossed on the breast, brought around the back, crossed there, and brought around again to the front and tied. Recommendations vary from at least three feet to six feet in length.[6] The material for these tapes is not prescribed; they may be of any color and material.[7] Only one ornament is mentioned by the rubrics; in the center of the top part of the amice there should be a small cross which the celebrant kisses before he puts it on. Since this cross should be plainly visible, it should be sewn in place with colored thread.[8]

[3] Canon 1296, § 3; cf. *supra*, pp. 4-9.

[4] Collins, *The Church Edifice*, p. 223.

[5] Anson, *Churches*, p. 195; Collins, *The Church Edifice*, p. 223; J. O'Connell, *The Celebration of Mass*, I, 262.

[6] Collins, *op. cit., loc. cit.*; Anson, *op. cit.*, p. 200; J. O'Connell, *op. cit., loc. cit.*

[7] J. O'Connell, *op. cit., loc. cit.*

[8] J. O'Connell, *op. cit.*, loc. cit.

The alb is a long white garment with close-fitting sleeves. It completely covers the cassock of the celebrant; it should reach nearly to the ground; the rubrics of the *Missal* note that the wearer is to adjust it in such manner that it hangs about a finger's breadth from the ground.[9] The authors note that there are two kinds of albs now generally in use: one type is made in such a way that the upper part of it fits the upper part of the body while the lower part of the alb flares out by means of gussets inserted under the arms or at the waist; the other type, called the "sack" alb, is the same width at the top and bottom.[10] It is this latter type which appears to be most commonly used in the United States; it is recommended as most practical, because it can be worn by any priest "no matter what his build."[11] Albs are fastened at the top either by means of strings or with a button. "An alb is more practical if fastened at the neck with a button; tapes have a way of getting into a knot."[12] There are also albs which have neither of these types of fastenings, but which have only an opening sufficiently large for the alb to be passed over the head. J. O'Connell recommends this type as a better form.[13]

The size of the alb, of course, depends upon each wearer. "The ideal would be that each priest have his own alb made to his measurements."[14]

Collins recommends the following average measurements for albs:

> 58 inches long, neck to hem:
> sleeve, 24 inches long, 24 inches in circumference, narrowing to 16 inches around cuff. Circumference around hem, 4 yards. Shoulder yokes, 5 x 8 inches; neckband, 20 x 1 inches across back in diameter. Depth of front placket, 13½ inches. Tapes, 20 x ½ inches each. Under-arm gussets, 5½ x 5½ inches.[15]

---

[9] *Loc. cit.* Cf. Francis, *The Laws of Holy Mass* (New York: Sheed and Ward, 1949), p. 87.

[10] Anson, *Churches*, p. 200; J. O'Connell, *The Celebration of Mass*, I, 262.

[11] J. O'Connell, *op. cit., loc. cit.*

[12] Anson, *Churches*, p. 200.

[13] *Op. cit., loc. cit.*

[14] Collins, *The Church Edifice*, p. 225.

[15] *Loc. cit.*

The proper and suitable ornamentation or decoration of the alb has been the subject of several decrees of the S.R.C. These dealt with decorations which appear on the cuffs or the bottom part of the alb. Ordinarily, ornamentation takes one of three forms: embroidery, lace, and foundations.

Regarding the first kind of ornamentation, embroidery, the S.R.C. has issued only one decree. In that decree it ruled that it is permissible to use albs which have embroidery on the cuffs and on the lower part of the skirt.[16]

The use of lace as an ornamentation of the alb is permitted by several decrees of the S.R.C. The earliest decree on this matter permits the use of lace in which are represented crosses, ostensoria, chalices with the host, figures of angels, and other sacred objects of a similar nature.[17] A later decree permits canons to use albs with lace skirts on the more solemn occasions.[18] Likewise, the decree which permits the use of embroidery also includes permission to use lace.[19] Indirect approval of the use of lace on the alb is given in that decree which approves the use of foundations.[20]

Colored foundations are also permitted as an ornamentation for the alb. In the first decree given on the matter, no specific color was mentioned.[21] The second decree approved the custom of using blue foundations on the cuffs and skirt.[22] The latest decrees on the proper color of foundations states that regularly the color should correspond to the color of the cuffs and bottom of the cassock which each celebrant or minister is entitled to wear.[23] Hence

[16] S.R.C., *Romana,* 12 iul. 1892, ad V—*Decr. Auth.,* n. 3780.

[17] S.R.C., *Syren.,* 5 dec. 1868, ad V—*Decr. Auth.,* n. 3191. Wapelhorst says of such ornamentation: *"Certe etiam minus convenit habere reticulum cum objectis vel figuris sacris, praesertim in inferiori parte Albae, quia hae figurae in geneflectendo conculcantur, quod indecentiam sapit." Compendium Sacrae Liturgiae,* n. 34.

[18] S.R.C., *Goana,* 16 iun. 1893, ad 12—*Decr. Auth.,* n. 3804.

[19] S.R.C., *Romana,* 12 iul. 1892, ad V—*Decr. Auth.,* n. 3780.

[20] S.R.C., *Minoricen.,* 24 nov. 1899, ad VII—*Decr. Auth.,* n. 4048.

[21] S.R.C., *Romana,* 12 iul. 1892, ad V—*Decr. Auth.,* n. 3780.

[22] S.R.C., *Minoricen.,* 24 nov. 1899, ad VII—*Decr. Auth.,* n. 4048.

[23] S.R.C., *Bergomen.,* 25 maii 1906, ad III—*Decr. Auth.,* n. 4186.

it appears that the proper colors for foundations would be: "black for a simple priest, violet for a prelate, red for a cardinal."[24]

Although the use of lace as an ornamentation for the alb is quite clearly tolerated by the S.R.C., and tradition, furthermore, appears to sanction such a use, the trend in recent times is away from such ornamentation. Such, too, is the sentiment of modern authors on the subject. J. O'Connell states:

> Lace on an alb is an accessory, and must not become the chief thing; it should not become too deep for this reason, and also because the use of lace on ecclesiastical garments is a sign of rank. Lace is, too, a sign of festivity, and so an entirely plain alb should be worn on ordinary days and for penitential seasons.[25]

Anson gives a more practical reason, namely, that "open-work lace albs are often dangerous garments, especially if too long for the wearer, for it is easy for him to put his foot through the lace." He likewise notes that the use of lace is a sign of rank, and not really suitable for ordinary priests.[26] Wapelhorst is particularly vehement in his condemnation of cheap lace: *"nam (et in hoc habetur abusus) non amplius e pretiosa materia ornatus Albae consistit, sed e vili omnimode textura."*[27]

There is also one other form of decoration or ornamentation for the alb noted by authors, namely, apparels.[28] These are usually pieces of colored brocade or other rich material tacked lightly around the cuffs or the skirt of the alb; they are generally four to six inches in diameter. Sometimes, too, they are strips of material embroidered in rather bright colors. There is no reason why the apparels should conform to the color of the vestment which the priests is at the time wearing. From a practical point of view, they are an effective ornament because they can be easily detached from the alb and washed. While neither the liturgical books nor the De-

[24] J. O'Connell, *The Celebration of Mass,* I, 263.

[25] *The Celebration of Mass,* I, 263.

[26] *Churches,* p. 200.

[27] *Compendium Sacrae Liturgiae,* n. 34.

[28] Cf. Anson, *Churches,* p. 208; fn. 30; J. O'Connell, *The Celebration of Mass,* I, 263.

crees of the S.R.C. mention apparels as a form of decoration for the alb, still it appears that they are a permissible form of decoration.

The modern trend towards plain white albs, or albs ornamented with a strip of embroidery some four or five inches wide, or with a lace insertion of a similar width, seems to be more in keeping with the dignity of the liturgy. Such albs are certainly more becoming than those which have a skirt made entirely of cheap, machine-made lace net-work type of material.

The material of the amice and alb, though not specified in the rubrics of the *Missal* or the *Ceremonial,* must be linen or hemp. A general Decree of the S.R.C., issued on May 15, 1819, orders that albs and amices are to be made only of linen or hemp; all other materials are excluded as unsuitable, even though they may vie and be equal to linen and hemp in their tidy neatness, their shining whiteness, and their tensile strength.[29]

The General Decree of 1819 gave some consideration towards those churches which had cotton vestments on hand; permission was granted for the wearing until they were worn out, of such cotton amices and albs as were already in use; there was, however, the added specification that, once these cotton vestments were worn out, they were to be replaced only with linen or hempen ones. Since 1819 similar concessions have at various times been granted for the use of non-linen or non-hempen albs until they were worn out.[30]

The Congregation of Rites has applied the General Decree of 1819 to new materials. With two exceptions, it has refused to yield even in the face of apparent great poverty on the part of the church. There was the case of the pastor in the Diocese of Ascoli Picano who had taken over a parish and found that it was entirely without these vestments; the income of the parish did not admit the purchase of new albs or amices made of linen and hemp. How-

[29] S.R.C., *decr. gen.,* 15 maii 1819—*Decr. Auth.,* n. 2600. This decree received the direct approbation of the Holy Father, who further directed that ordinaries see to its observance.

[30] S.R.C., *Hieracen.,* 12 mart. 1836—*Decr. Auth.,* n. 2737; *Goana,* 23 iul. 1878; ad II—*Decr. Auth.,* n. 3455; *Lauden.,* 23 iun. 1892, ad II—*Decr. Auth.,* n. 3779; *Placentina in Hispania,* 13 aug. 1895, ad II—*Decr. Auth.,* n. 3868.

ever, this pastor himself had a considerable quantity of material fabricated from ramie (*ex urticis confecta*). It was his desire to make the necessary vestments from this material. In spite of these extraordinary circumstances, the S.R.C. gave a negative answer and commanded that the General Decree be observed.[31]

In like manner, in 1895, the S.R.C. replied in the negative to a request to make albs and amices from another type of material called "*Nipis.*" The request noted that this material was not unlike linen in its fabrication, that is to say, it was made of the stem of the plant just as linen is, rather than from the fruit of the plant as cotton is; that it was much more valuable than cotton.[32]

There are, however, as was noted above, two exceptions on record in which the S.R.C. granted permission to use material other than linen or hemp for the amice and alb. The first was granted to the Vicariate Apostolic of Suchow in China. This was a permission to make amices and albs from a material called "*Hiapou,*" which seems to be the same as, or at least very similar to, the material already mentioned which was made of ramie. In view of the extraordinary circumstances enumerated in the request, the S.R.C. granted the Vicariate a dispensation from the general law, which requires that these vestments be made of linen or hemp, to make them in the future from "*Hiapou.*"[33]

More recently the S.R.C. granted permission to the Bishop of Vicenza to use a material fabricated from ramie for the manufacture of amices and albs.[34]

These particular concessions on the part of the S.R.C., however, appear to be actual indults or dispensations in particular cases, and therefore cannot be extended beyond those places in whose favor they have been granted. Rather, they serve to show that the intent of the S.R.C. is that linen and hemp are the only suitable materials for amices and albs.

[31] S.R.C., *Asculana in Piceno,* 17 dec. 1875—*Decr. Auth.,* n. 3387.

[32] S.R.C.,*Placentina in Hispania,* 13 aug. 1895—*Decr. Auth.,* n. 3868.

[33] S.R.C.,*Se-Ciuensis, Sept.—Occidentalis,* 27 iun. 1898—*Decr. Auth.,* n. 3995.

[34] *Coll. Decr.,* n. 82. No date is given in the rescript itself as recorded in this work; the latter notes that it appeared in *Ephem. lit., IP,* 56 (1942), 30.

Although there are no decrees regarding the use of silk, rayon, and nylon for the use of albs, it appears that these must be considered proscribed materials for amices and albs. This seems quite clear from the attitude taken thus far by the S.R.C. rergarding the introduction of new materials for this purpose, as well as from the words of the General Decree of 1819: *"non autem ex alia quacumque materia, etsi munditie, candore ac tenacitate linum aut cannabem aemulante et aequante.*

Some question could be raised regarding the material of the ornamentation of albs, especially in those cases where lace is used. Capello is of the opinion that, as long as the ornamentation does not comprise the greater portion of the alb, it may be made of any material at all, which if it does comprise a major portion of the alb, such ornamentation must be made of linen.[35] Wapelhorst, quoting Van der Stappen, makes no such distinction. He states quite simply that lace which is made of cotton is unsuitable and prohibited material for the ornamentation of albs.[36] Inasmuch as no decree has been issued by the S.R.C. on the material of the decoration of albs, Cappelo's opinion seems to be in accord with the law.

B. ***Cincture***

Neither the rubrics nor the decrees of the S.R.C. specify the proper material for the cincture. The latter, however, indicate that linen is the more appropriate material. In a decree, in 1701, the S.R.C. replied that it was more proper to use linen cinctures than silk ones.[37] From this decree it is generally deduced that silk cinctures are permissible, but should be reserved for prelates.[38] The S.R.C. has also ruled that the use of woolen cinctures is permissible.[39]

The cincture should be in the form of a cord, and not in the form of a sash or band.[40] Ordinarily, the cinctures are white; however,

[35] *De Sacramentis,* I, n. 757.

[36] *Compendium Sacrae Liturgiae,* n. 34.

[37] S.R.C., *Cong. Montis Coronae,* 22 ian. 1701, ad 7—*Decr. Auth.,* n. 2067.

[38] Anson, *Churches,* p. 201; J. O'Connell, *The Celebration of Mass,* I, 263.

[39] S.R.C., *Cong. Ordinis Carthusianorum,* 23 dec. 1862—*Decr. Auth.,* n. 3118.

[40] S.R.C., *Minoricen.,* 24 nov. 1899, ad VI—*Decr. Auth.,* n. 4048.

it is licit to use cinctures which conform to the colors of the vestments.[41] Since the cincture is worn double, and since after girding it has loose ends which are to be used to fasten the ends of the stole, it is recommended that the cincture be from four to four and one half yards long.[42] The ends of the cincture are usually finished off in tassels or fringes.

ARTICLE II: THE OUTER VESTMENTS *(Paramenta)*: MANIPLE, STOLE, CHASUBLE

A. *Material*

Although neither the rubrics of the Liturgical Books nor any general decrees of the Sacred Congregation of Rites have specified the proper material for the manufacture of the outer vestments, all the Decrees of the S.R.C. which have dealt with the matter point to but three materials as suitable and licit. These materials are silk, cloth of gold, and cloth of silver. This conclusion is reached, not in view of the fact that the S.R.C. has specified that such materials are proper, but rather by a process of elimination and intimation, that is to say, in view of the fact that other materials have been proscribed, and these have thus become approved indirectly. The authors, too, are unanimous in their opinion that only silk, gold, or silver vestments are licit.[43]

That cloth of gold and cloth of silver are considered suitable materials is apparent, not from direct decrees regarding the material, but rather from those decrees which give rulings with regard to the colors of the vestment. Thus, having been asked whether vestments which were made almost entirely *("maxima saltem parte")* of gold could be used for all colors except violet and black, the S.R.C. replied that the custom of the place was to be tolerated in this respect only with regard to those vestments which were made

41 S.R.C., *Bracharen.*, 8 iun. 1709, ad 3—*Decr. Auth.*, n. 2194.

42 J. O'Connell, *The Celebration of Mass,* I, 264.

43 Cappello, *De Sacramentis,* I, n. 759; Collins, *The Church Edifice,* p. 229; Gasparri, *De SS. Eucharistia,* n. 692; J. O'Connell, *The Celebration of Mass,* I, 259; L. O'Connell, *The Book of Ceremonies,* p. 23; Wapelhorst, *Compendium Sacrae Liturgiae,* n. 38.

of gold.[44] In two other decrees the S.R.C. gave the same ruling, namely, that gold vestments may be used for all the colors except violet and black.[45] In like manner it ruled that silver vestments can be used in place of white ones.[46]

That silk, gold, and silver are regarded as the only suitable materials for these vestments becomes more apparent when one studies the decrees which proscribed or forbade the use of any other type of material. Thus the use of linen or cotton vestments is forbidden in a decree that was issued to the diocese of Modena.[47] This decree noted the rubrics and the usage *(usus omnium Ecclesiarum)* of all the churches should be observed, and then stated that these did not admit such chasubles.

A new type of material, the primary feature of which was glass thread which was mixed with silk, gold,or silver, was also proscribed.[48] In like manner the S.R.C. has given a ruling that woolen vestments may not be used.[49]

Hence it is clear that the S.R.C. considers cotton, linen, and wool to be unsuitable materials for the manufacture of vestments. This attitude of the S.R.C. is well summed up in its warning *(monitum)* of 1881. In effect this warning was: In spite of the fact that the Sacred Congregation of Rites had frequently declared as illicit the use of chasubles and other similar vestments made of cotton, linen, or wool, nonetheless some manufacturers of these materials were selling vestments of such materials in such a way as to indicate that these materials were permitted by the Sacred Congregation of Rites. In order to ward off any false opinion in so important a matter, the ordinaries were reminded that the decrees of the S.R.C. with regard to the materials of the vestments were still fully in effect, and that there was no recent disposition which in any way modified those decrees.[50]

44 S.R.C., *Guadalaxara,* 28 apr. 1866—*Decr. Auth.,* n. 3145.

45 S.R.C., *Syren.,* 5 dec. 1868, ad IV—*Decr. Auth.,* n. 3191; *Papien.,* 20 nov. 1885, ad II—*Decr. Auth.,* n. 3646.

46 S.R.C., *Papien,* 20 nov. 1885, ad III—*Decr. Auth.,* n. 3646.

47 S.R.C., *Mutinen.,* 23 sept. 1837, ad V, n. 3—*Decr. Auth.,* n. 2769.

48 S.R.C., *Atrebaten.,* 11 sept. 1847—*Decr. Auth.,* n. 2949.

49 S.R.C., *Lauden.,* 23 iun. 1892, ad I—*Decr. Auth.,* n. 3543.

50 *ASS,* XIV (1881), 144.

The mind of the S.R.C. that silk is the ordinary material for vestments is also apparent from two decrees which permit the manufacture of vestments which are made of materials mixed with silk. The first such decree permits the use of vestments the outer surface of which is made of silk mixed with cotton, wool, or linen, but which appears as silk to the eye.[51] The second decree permits the use of a material which is a texture of silk and of threads of the cloth-mulberry. In granting permission to use this material, the S.R.C. stipulated that the texture should not be changed through the addition of any other material.[52] It should be noted that in both cases the permitted material is at least partly silk.

There is only one decree which appears to give a specific ruling that only silk, gold, and silver are suitable materials for vestments. This again came as an indirect ruling on the material. The primary point concerned ornamentation. It was asked whether it was licit to use vestments on which pictures were painted; the pictures themselves were done on linen or cotton, which was then glued to the vestment. The decree rules that such vestments may be used provided that the vestments proper are made of silk, gold, or silver, and made in accord with liturgical law (*dummodo agatur de paramentis sericis, vel auro argentoque contextis, ac de cetero ad normam legum liturgicarum confectis*).[53]

Hence it appears to be perfectly permissible to conclude that at the present time the only materials which can be used licitly for the manufacture of the outer vestments are silk, gold, and silver. It should be noted here, too, that in the case of gold and silver, the material to be used is not gold-colored, or silver-colored material, but material which is actually made of gold or silver thread.[54] Moreover, in view of the fact that gold vestments are permitted in place of silk ones because of the precious, i.e., value of the gold thread (*causa pretiositatis*),[55] imitation gold, e.g., vestments of copper or of brass are illicit.

[51] S.R.C., *Gnesen, et Ponanien.*, 23 mart. 1882—*Decr. Auth.*, n. 3543.

[52] S.R.C., *Ceneten.*, 21 apr. 1893—*Decr. Auth.*, n. 3796.

[53] S.R.C., *Brunen.*, 30 mart. 1885—*Decr. Auth.*, n. 3628.

[54] S.R.C., *Adrien.*, 29 mart. 1851, ad 5—*Decr. Auth.*, n. 2968.

[55] S.R.C., *Papien.*, 20 nov. 1885, ad II et III—*Decr. Auth.*, n. 3646.

Until the present, at least, the S.R.C. has given no ruling regarding vestments made of nylon. Until a decree is forthcoming on the matter, it appears to be illicit to use this material for vestments, even though it is generally regarded to have the same appearance, texture, and value as silk.

B. *Ornamentation*

The rubrics require that the maniple and stole be marked with a cross which the celebrant kisses before he dons these vestments.[56] The ends of the maniple and stole are usually ornamented with a fringe or with tassling.[57] There is one other prescription in the liturgical books about the ornamentation of the outer vestments. The *Ceremonial* directs that in Masses for the dead all of the vestments, whether of the altar, of the celebrant, of the ministers, of the books, or of the faldstool, are to be black, and that no images of the dead along with the white crosses are to be placed on them.[58] The S.R.C. has ruled that this rubric rules out the use of a representation of the skull and cross bones on the vestments.[59]

Apart from these prescriptions, there appear to be practically no limitations on the ornamentation of the vestments. Thus the S.R.C. tolerates the use of flowers and foliage, either embroidered or painted on the vestment.[60] Another licit type of decoration is the use of pictures of the Saints.[61] However, the decorations must conform in color to the color of the particular vestment. That is to say, the ornamentation is not to be such as will obscure the proper color of the vestment. One color must be plainly predominate.[62]

The material of the ornamentation is not prescribed. It appears that any material is suitable for this purpose.[63] It does not have

[56] *Missale Romanum,* Tit. *Ritus servandus in celebratione Missae,* Cap. I, n. 3.

[57] J. O'Connell, *The Celebration of Mass,* I, 264-265.

[58] Lib. II, Cap. XI, n. 1.

[59] S.R.C., *Dubiorum,* 24 nov. 1905, ad I—*Decr. Auth.,* n. 4174.

[60] S.R.C., *Cuneen.,* 2 iun. 1883, ad XV—*Decr. Auth.,* n. 3576.

[61] S.R.C., *Brunen.,* 30 mart. 1885—*Decr. Auth.,* n. 3628.

[62] S.R.C., *Marsorum.;* 12 nov. 1831, ad 50—*Decr. Auth.,* n. 2682; *Mutinen.,* 23 sept. 1837, ad V, n. 2—*Decr. Auth.,* n. 2769.

[63] J. O'Connell, *The Celebration of Mass,* I, 263.

to be silk, silver or gold. This is also evident from the response of the S.R.C. which permits the use of pictures painted on cotton or linen and then glued to the vestment proper.[64]

C. *Color of the Outer Vestments*

> *Paramenta Altaris, Celebrantis et Ministrorom debent esse coloris convenientis Officio et Missae diei, secundum usum Romanae Ecclesiae: quae quinque coloribus uti consuevit, Albo, Rubeo, Viridi, Violaceo et Nigro.*[65]

The matter of the proper colors for the outer vestments is quite clearly stated in this rubric of the *Missal.* They are white, red, green, violet, and black, together with rose which is prescribed by the *Ceremonial* and the S.R.C. for the third Sunday of Advent and the fourth Sunday in Lent.[66] Two decrees of the S.R.C. emphasize that vestments must conform to the liturgical colors.[67] Even the more precious vestments are not to be used on the more solemn days if they do not conform to the liturgical color of the days in question.[68]

The practice of using yellow vestments for all colors except violet or black has come to the attention of the S.R.C. on numerous occasions. The Congregation has consistently given the answer that yellow vestments are not to be so used.[69] In fact, yellow vestments are not to be used at all. Yellow is not one of the liturgical colors; nor can it be said to be a substitute for gold vestments, which, as will be pointed out, may be used for other colors.[70] Blue

[64] S.R.C., *Brunen.*, 30 mart. 1885—*Decr. Auth.*, n. 3628.

[65] *Missale Romanum,* Tit. *Rubricae Generales Missae,* Cap. XVIII, *De Coloribus Paramentorum,* n. 1. The rest of the numbers of this chapter prescribe at which times the various colors are to be used.

[66] *Caeremoniale Episcoporum,* Lib. II, Cap. XIII, n. 11; S.R.C., *Vallis Vidonis,* 29 nov. 1901, ad III—*Decr. Auth.*, n. 4084.

[67] S.R.C., *Vicen.*, 19 dec. 1829—*Decr. Auth.*, n. 2675; *Marsorum.*, 12 nov. 1831, ad 50—*Decr. Auth.*, n. 2682.

[68] *Decr. Auth.*, n. 2682.

[69] S.R.C., *Marsorum.*, 12 nov. 1831, ad 50—*Decr. Auth.*, n. 2682; *Mutinen.*, 23 sept. 1837, ad V, n. 1—*Decr. Auth.*, n. 2769; *Syren.*, 5 dec. 1868, ad IV—*Decr. Auth.*, n. 3191.

[70] S.R.C., *Veronen.*, 16 mart. 1833, ad 4—*Decr. Auth.*, n. 2704; *Lauden.*, 23 iun. 1892, ad III—*Decr. Auth.*, n. 3779.

is also an unliturgical color, and accordingly is not to be used.[71]

Multi-colored vestments are not allowed; that is to say, vestments which have such a mixture of colors (even though individually none is out of accord with the rubrics) that it is impossible to point to any predominant color. Further, even though the rubrical color or colors can be discerned in such vestments, it is not permissible to use them in place of white, green, red or violet vestments.[72]

Gold-colored vestments are also proscribed.[73] It is possible that the practice (observable even today) of using gold-colored vestments in place of white, red, or green, is due to the fact that the use of gold vestments for all the colors except violet and black is licit.[74] However, it must be noted again that in the use of gold vestments it is not the color of the material which is to be considered, but rather the fact that the material itself must be made of gold, and not merely be gold-colored.[75] It is permissible to use silver vestments in place of white ones.[76]

By way of summary one may state that the Decrees of the S.R.C. constantly insist on the use of only the rubrical colors, white, red, green, violet, and black. Vestments made of gold or silver material may be used. All other colors, especially gold-color, yellow, and blue are specifically proscribed as illicit.

[71] S.R.C., *Veronen.*, 16 mart. 1833, ad 4—*Decr. Auth.*, n. 2704; *Congregationis Oblatorum B.V.M.*, 23 febr. 1839, ad 2—*Decr. Auth.*, n. 2788. It may be noted, however, that an Apostolic indult was granted to the Spanish Kingdom to use blue vestments for the feast of the Immaculate Conception and for votive Masses of the Immaculate Conception. The indult, however, did not extend to other feasts of the Blessed Virgin, even though they might in some way be related to the Immaculate Conception, such as the Apparition of Lourdes or the Feast of Our Lady of the Miraculous Medal.—*ASS*, XXXIV (1902), 555-556.

[72] S.R.C., *Mutinen.*, 23 sept. 1837, ad V, n. 2—*Decr. Auth.*, n. 2769.

[73] S.R.C., *Adrien.*, 29 mart. 1851, ad 5—*Decr. Auth.*, n. 2986.

[74] S.R.C., *Guadalaxara*, 28 apr. 1866—*Decr. Auth.*, n. 3145; *Syren.*, 5 dec. 1868, ad IV—*Decr. Auth.*, n. 3191; *Papien.*, 20 nov. 1885, ad II—*Decr. Auth.*, n. 3646.

[75] Cf. *supra.*, p. 140.

[76] S.R.C., *Papien.*, 20 nov. 1885, ad III—*Decr. Auth.*, n. 3646.

D. *Form of the Outer Vestments*

1. Manipule and Stole

There as no rubrics in the Liturgical Books or in the Decrees of the S.R.C. which specify the proper form of maniple and stole. At the present time there are two types of maniples in use: one which has the same width (usually about three inches) for its entire length; the other which widens out to some five or six inches at the end. The latter type is the kind which most conforms to Roman usage.[77] It is recommended that the maniple be made of flexible rather than stiffened material.[78] Moreover, it should be long enough to prevent its end from touching the corporal when the priest raises or joins his hands. The length recommended is 38 to 48 inches in all, so that the half length is 19 to 24 inches.[79]

Two types of fasteners are ordinarily in use for keeping the maniple in place on the arm of the priest: the most common one seems to be the small tab with which the maniple is pinned to the sleeve of the alb; the other consists of a band of elastic attached on the inside surface of the maniple. The two sides of the maniple are usually joined together at a point near the top in such a way as to obtain an opening large enough to permit the priest to put his arm through it. J. O'Connell notes that if this is done on both sides, it permits the priest to wear the maniple without the use of fasteners.[80]

As is the case with the maniple, two types of stoles are in use today: the one, which is of the same width (about three inches) for its entire length; the other, which widens out to five or six inches at the ends. In construction, too, stoles are made in two ways—either in one piece, i.e., quite straight, or in two pieces joined together in the center at an angle which make the stole lie more smoothly under the chasuble. J. O'Connell states that the stole should be quite long, at least 9 to 10 feet in its undoubled

[77] Anson, *Churches,* p. 188; J. O'Connell, *The Celebration of Mass,* I. 264.

[78] Anson, *op. cit., loc. cit.;* J. O'Connell, *op. cit., loc. cit.;* Collins, *The Church Edifice,* p. 232; L. O'Connell, *The Book of Ceremonies,* p. 24.

[79] J. O'Connell, *op. cit.,* I, p. 264, fn. 9.

[80] *Op. cit.,* I, p. 264, fn. 11.

length for the following reasons: it should extend below the chasuble; it is to be "placed between the shoulders (and not around the neck), . . . and then crossed in front."[81] Anson concurs with J. O'Connell in this opinion that the stole is to be placed between the shoulders rather than around the neck, and for this reason says: "It is unnecessary to sew on a piece of linen (the linen is a relic of times when priests wore their hair long) or lace in the middle."[82] If, on the contrary, the stole is worn around the neck, as seems to be the custom in the United States, such a piece of linen will be no small aid in preventing the stole from becoming soiled.[83]

2. Chasuble

Just as the rubrics of the Liturgical Books and the Decrees of the S.R.C. are silent about the proper form of the maniple and the stole, so too are they silent about the proper form of the chasuble, with the exception of one Decree of the S.R.C.[84] This decree of 1925 has caused no little concern regarding what is called variously the "gothic," "semi-gothic," "revival gothic," "ample," or "oval" form of the chasuble. It appears that this form of vestment was gaining considerable popularity; the Decree of 1925 raises the question of the lawfulness of the use of this type of vestment. For the sake of clarity in discussing the matter, it seems wise to give a brief history of the development of the chasuble; then to quote the Decree of 1925 in full; and finally to consider the opinions that have been ventured on the matter.

a. Historical notes on the chasuble

At one time it was supposed that the primitive chasuble was completely round, so that, if laid flat on the ground it would form a circular disk. Subsequent research has

---

[81] *The Celebration of Mass,* I, 264.

[82] *Churches,* p. 187.

[83] Regarding the proper way to wear the stole, it may be noted that the *Missal* states: "et imponit medium eius in collo." Cf. Tit. *Ritus Servandus in Celebratione Missae,* Cap. I, n. 3. Francis translates this as: "and places the middle of it on his neck." *The Laws of Holy Mass,* p. 87.

[84] *Dubium,* 9 dec. 1925—*Decr. Auth.,* n. 4398.

> made it clear that the original "little house" was invariably bell-shaped, i.e., rather like a cope with the front edges joined. In fact, the two garments were in origin the same. The open form of (the cope) was found more convenient as a rain cloak! The chasuble would have been made out of a semicircle of cloth with the straight edge folded over in the middle and the two borders sewn together. Should the garment have been made of any heavy material it would have been awkward because of the weight on the arms.
>
> During the Middle Ages when heavier fabrics became more common and embroidery more elaborate, it was almost impossible for the priest to raise his hands or arms unless the deacon or subdeacon were at his side to roll back the chasuble. So, by degrees the chasuble was lightened by cutting it away on the arms; the length in front and behind remaining practically unaltered for many centuries. This process of shortening and cutting away the sides to secure greater freedom of movement went on from the thirteenth to the seventeenth century, until the chasuble lost all trace of its original cloak form and assumed the appearance of two stiffened panels joined by shoulder straps, rather like a modern "sandwich man's" boards . . .
>
> There are several types of the post-Reformation chasubles which were evolved during the seventeenth and eighteenth centuries—Italian, French, German, and Spanish. The Italian (usually called "Roman") is rectangular shaped at the back, extending just beyond the edge of the shoulders and cut away in front, rather like a fiddle . . . The French chasuble is shorter and stiffer . . . the Spanish type is longer than either the French or Italian, but is more cut away on the shoulders, so that from behind, the bottom appears to be wider than the top.[85]

It should be noted here that, regardless of their national origin, modern chasubles have one thing in common, the cutaway sides.

b. The Decree of 1925

The Sacred Congregation of Rites was asked:

> Whether in the manufacture and use of vestments for

---

85 Anson, *Churches,* p. 190.

the Sacrifice of the Mass and Sacred Functions, it is permitted to depart from the usage which is received in the Church, and to introduce a different mode and form, even though it be ancient.

Reply. The S.C. Rit., after having heard from the Code Commission, replied: It is not permitted without applying to the Holy See; according to the Decree or Letter of the S.C. Rit. to the Ordinaries under date of 21 Aug., 1863.

The above reply was approved by His Holiness.

Note: The Letter referred to in the Reply is as follows:

Whereas it is known to the Holy See upon information from certain Most Reverend Bishops and other ecclesiastical and lay persons, that some dioceses in England, France, Germany, and Belgium have changed the form of the vestments used in the most holy Sacrifice of the Mass, and modeled them according to the so-called "Gothic" style, in a rather artistic fashion, the Sacred Congregation which has the charge and guardianship of legitimate rites has made a thorough investigation of this change.

And from this investigation, although the Sacred Congregation well knows that those sacred vestments in the Gothic style were in common use especially in the thirteenth, fourteenth, and fifteenth centuries, yet, mindful also of the fact that the Roman Church and other Churches of the Latin rite throughout the world, without objection from the Holy See, have from the sixteenth century, that is, from about the time of the Council of Trent, up until our own times, abandoned their use, the Sacred Congregation has decided that while the present discipline continues, no change should be made without consulting the Holy See, as the Sovereign Pontiffs have more than once announced in their Constitutions, wisely declaring that such changes, being contrary to the approved practice of the Church, can often cause disturbance and produce astonishment in the minds of the faithful. At the same time, because the Sacred Congregation of Rites believes that there may be reasons of some weight in favor of the present change, it has decided, after consultation with His Holiness, Pius XI, to extend to Your Amplitude a most gracious invitation to state the reasons which have given rise to these changes, in as far as such changes have taken place in your diocese.[86]

A first reading of this Decree together with the accompanying letter appears to make it very clear that the so-called "Gothic" style of vestments, in fact that no new or different style of vestment, is to be introduced without a previous consulting of the Holy See. Indeed, many authors are satisfied with this brief comment on the Decree.[87] However, as Anson observes, there is a difference of opinion as to the meaning of the Decree. "However," he says, "most authorities are agreed that it rules out all forms of vestments which are not based on those *actually* worn in Rome—unless previous permission has been obtained to re-introduced vestments of an earlier shape."[88] He does not, however, make mention of who these authorities are.

Pauwels is of the opinion that such chasubles may be used until they are worn out.[89] His opinion, however, is that the new chasubles of this type should not be obtained without the previous permission of the Holy See.[90] He further states: *"Novimus iam non uni ecclesiae concessam esse ut casulae gothicae adhiberi possent saltem donec usu tritae non essent."*[91] As a final touch one may add Pauwel's statement that art lovers can legitimately hope that perhaps some time in the future the S.R.C. will give its approval to ample vestments.[92]

Even Roulin, who is very much in favor of gothic or ample vestments, and who devoted a full chapter entitled *Full Vestments*

86 Translation taken from Bouscaren, *The Canon Law Digest,* I, 374-375.

87 Coronata, *Inst. Iur. Can.,* II, n. 878; Wernz-Vidal, *Ius Canonicum,* Tom. IV, vol. 1, n. 429; Vermeersch-Creusen, *Epitome,* II, n. 624.

88 *Churches,* p. 185.

89 "De forma paramentorum," *Periodica de Religiosis et Missionariis* (Brugis, 1905-1919); *Periodica de Re Canonica et Morali utili praesertim Religiosis et Missionariis* (1920-1927); *Periodica de Re Canonica, Morali, Liturgica* (Brugis, 1928-1936; Romae, 1937—) (hereafter cited as *Periodica*), XV (1926-1927), 65.

90 *Loc. cit.*

91 "La forme des ornaments liturgiques," *Revue des Communautés Religieuses* (Louvain, 1925—), II, (1926), 77.

92 "La forme des chasubles," *Nouvelle Revue Théologique* (Paris, 1869—), LIII (1926), 304.

Lawful, Traditional and Beautiful to the defense of their use makes the following statement:

> These are the weighty considerations which their lordships the bishops will not fail to represent at Rome. They were invited to do so *"verbis amantissimis"* (in most cordial terms); and, as we hope, by means of indults and numerous approbations the full chasuble will come into ever wider and wider use.[93]

This is an admission on the part of one of the strongest proponents for full vestments that an indult or at least an approbation is necessary for their legal use.

J. O'Connell is of the opinion that the Decree of 1925 plainly forbids all churches of the Latin Rite to depart from the present received usage in Rome by introducing another style and shape of chasuble, even an old one.[94] He says specifically: "The more ample form of the chasuble (be it the primitive or the medieval type, or the modern Gothic-revival type) is not permitted without indult."[95] Footnote no. 34 on page 268 of J. O'Connell's work (Vol. I of his *The Celebration of Mass*) has been the occasion of a lengthy and scholarly refutation of this position by Joaquim Nabuco.[96]

J. O'Connell's footnote follows:

> Some writers, however, think that it is permitted, despite the clear terms of decree 4398. It seems to be the unanimous wish, not only of the lovers of sacred art, but also of the rubricians, that the Holy See may in the future permit, or at least tolerate, the restoration of the more ample medieval form of the chasuble.

Nabuco's comment on this passage is: "It seems that O'Connell gives the decree no. 4398 of the SRC an amplitude which it cannot profess to have."[97]

It should be borne in mind that the question is not whether

[93] Roulin, *Vestments and Vesture* (Westminster, Md.: The Newman Press, 1950), pp. 112-113.

[94] *The Celebration of Mass,* I, 267.

[95] *Op. cit.,* I, 268.

[96] "The Form of Vestments," *ER,* CVI (1942), 241-254.

[97] "The Form of Vestments," *ER,* CVI (1942), 241.

the type of vestments is a major question reserved to the Holy See, but rather whether in view of Decree 4398 larger vestments may be used without permission from the Holy See. Nabuco is of the opinion that such vestments may be used without permission from the Holy See. He bases his answer on the following points:

> 1) The Holy See has never (as yet) published measurements for vestments, so much so, that they have always been and still are changing.
>
> 2) There are at least five *formae receptae* in the Latin Church, besides the ampler chasubles.
>
> 3) The decree of 1925 is to be interpreted in a strict sense and applied to countries where the Roman form is in general use.
>
> 4) The law of the Church in regard to vestments is to found in canon 1296, §3. Hence the decree of 1925 is to be interpreted accordingly, as a canon is more important than an answer of a Sacred Congregation.
>
> 5) The larger, or gothic chasuble, is in use in the Latin Church because:
>
> a) It has been adopted by whole religious Orders . . .
>
> b) It has been officially permitted or adopted, by a great number of dioceses . . .
>
> c) Such vestments have been officially allowed in all the Roman catacombs. The *Collegium Cultorum Martyrum* wears them in the Vatican at their annual procession. Pius XI said Mass in Saint Peter's on 19 March, 1930 (five years after the decree) in a gothic chasuble. It may be alleged that the Pope is not personally bound to observe liturgical laws. Yes, but although not obliged, Popes usually follow our Lord's example and obey the laws they themselves made. So we may gather that the Pope's intention was to say a Roman Mass, in a Roman church, with Roman vestments.
>
> 6) It cannot be said that so many pious and God-fearing people—religious superiors, bishops, cardinals of the Holy Roman Church, the Pope himself, are infringing on the law. The conclusion one reaches is that the Holy See, aware of the existing use of gothic chasubles, and having kept silence during sixteen years, tolerates (at least) their use: *Qui tacet consentire videtur.*[98]

---

[98] Ibid., pp. 251-253.

The reader is probably aware that Nabuco is a rubricist of no small repute among moderns. He is the author of a lengthy and scholarly commentary on the Pontifical.[99] In the present case, however, it appears that his argument in favor of the use of ample vestments without the previous permission of the Holy See lacks conclusiveness. This becomes clearer when each point of his argument is separately evaluated.

Regarding the first point, that the Holy See has not yet given measurements for vestments, and that they have always been and still are changing, the first part of the statement is true; the second part that vestments are still changing seems to be precisely the point covered by the Decree, namely, that no changes be introduced without a previous consulting of the Holy See.

The second point observes that there are five *formae receptae* in the Latin Church. In his fuller explanation of this point earlier in the article, Nabuco contends that the Decree does not include all five forms, namely, Italian (Roman), French, German, Spanish and Portuguese, but includes only the Italian or Roman form as the *forma recepta.* This is based on the fact that the Decree as contained in the *Decreta Authentica* of the S.R.C. used the words *"ab usu in Ecclesia Romana recepto."* O'Connell, too, interprets this part of the Decree in the same way, i.e., that vestments must now conform to the present received usage of the Church in Rome.[100] It should be noted, however, that the Decree in its initial official publication in the *AAS,* XVIII (1926), 58, omitted the word *Romana,* that is to say, the latter text reads *"ab usu in Ecclesia recepto."* It seems that this latter form of the phrase is more in accord with the whole tone of the decree, which appears to condemn all innovations without previous consultation with the Holy See. Furthermore, all five forms may be said to be of the same style, namely, that the sides are cut away; this cutting away of the sides is the major difference between the ample vestment and the Roman vestment. The proper interpretation of this part of the Decree would rather include all five of these forms,

99 *Pontificalis Romani Expositio,* 3 vols., Pertopoli-Brazil: Sumptibus (Jitora Vozes Ltda., 1945).

100 *The Celebration of Mass,* I, 266-267.

that is to say, the *usus receptus* cannot be limited strictly in every detail to that used in the City of Rome. Gasparri pointed out that while there is some difference between the vestments used in France and the ones used in other countries, the difference is very slight, and that there is no objection to the use of French vestments in other countries, and vice versa.[101] This interpretation at least conforms to the letter attached to the Decree; this letter, it will be recalled, specifically mentioned England, France, Germany, and Belgium, places in which, according to Nabuco himself, the strictly Roman vestment is not used.[102]

The third point of his argument is to the effect that in virtue of the principle, *odiosa sunt restringenda,* the Decree is to be interpreted strictly; his conclusion then is: since the Decree uses the words *"ab usu in Ecclesia Romana recepto,"* the Decree is applicable only to those countries where the Roman form is in use, namely, in Italy, and possibly in Malta. That this is manifestly not the intention of the S.R.C. is apparent from the fact that the attached letter mentions specifically France, England, Germany, and Belgium, places in which the strictly Roman form was not in use. Such an interpretation in this case makes the S.R.C. contradict itself.

The fourth point of Nubuco's argument, that the Decree is to be interpreted in the light of canon 1296, §3, is not precise legal argumentation. It would be more precise to say that canon 1296, §3, is to be interpreted in the light of the Decree; the latter is actually an interpretation of that part of canon 1296, §3, which states that regarding the form of vestments, ecclesiastical tradition is to be followed. Authentic interpretation of the Code is to be left to the Commission established by the Holy See for the specific purpose of interpreting the Code.[103]

In the present case the Decree itself notes that the Code Commission was consulted, thereby at least intimating that it was an interpretation of the law of the Code. Furthermore, the Decree

[101] *De SS. Eucharistia,* n. 700.

[102] "The Form of Vestments," *ER,* CVI (1942), 250.

[103] Benedictus XV, motu proprio, *Cum iuris canonici Codicem,* 15 sept. 1917—*AAS,* IX (1917), 483.

has the approval of the Holy Father; this gives it more authority than attaches to bare decree of a Congregation. Furthermore, it should be noted that the S.R.C. holds a peculiar place among the Congregations in so far as the law is concerned; other Congregations have under the Code no right to legislate or to interpret authentically.[104] By the Code itself the S.R.C. is charged with the supervision and regulation of all matters pertaining directly to the sacred rites and ceremonies of the Church.[105] Pope Pius XII in his recent Encyclical on the liturgy notes: "This body [S.R.C.] fulfills even today the official function of supervision and legislation with regard to all matters touching the sacred Liturgy."[106] Hence, one is actually faced with the question: what is the proper interpretation of Decree 4398?

Nabuco suggests that for a proper understanding of the Decree one should study canon 1296, §3. In so doing he concludes that there are no liturgical prescriptions with regard to the style of the vestments. Secondly, he concludes that the laws of sacred art are better observed in the ample vestment than in the Roman vestment. This is, of course, ultimately a matter of taste, i.e., to decide which style of vestment is the more beautiful. In this section, too, he argues that the ample vestment is more practical because of its greater flexibility. Arguments of practicality could also be advanced for the Roman form, e.g., the ample form of vestment, draping over the arms, makes it difficult to trace signs of the cross over the chalice, if not also dangerous; it makes opening and closing the tabernacle more difficult; oftentimes, when worn by a tall priest, the bottom part of an ample chasuble can sweep across the corporal at the elevation, while when worn by a very short priest it sweeps the ground at the times of profound bows and genuflexions.

Canon 1296, §3, specifies that in the style of the vestments, ecclesiastical tradition is to be followed. This is the precise crux of the matter: What is ecclesiastical tradition regarding the

[104] *Loc. cit.*
[105] Canon 253, §1.
[106] Encycl. *Mediator Dei,* n. 57.

vestments? Nabuco makes this ecclesiastical tradition derive from the opinion of the authors. Those whom he cites want ample vestments. The Letter attached to the Decree states specifically that the introduction of the so-called "Gothic" style is contrary to the approved practice of the Church. Hence tradition in this matter is not what the authors want, but rather what the actual practice of the Church is.

In footnote 26 on p. 251 of his article, Nabuco quotes that part of canon 23 which states that *"leges posteriores ad priores trahendae sunt et his in quantum fieri potest conciliandae."* Admitting that in the matter under discussion there is a doubt, one must have recourse to pre-Code law.

The history of the letter of 1863 according to Nabuco is as follows: The occasion of the letter was a visit of Msgr. Corazza, papal master of ceremonies, and as such a consultor to the S.R.C. On this visit to Belgium and Germany he saw a considerable number of ample chasubles. On returning to Rome he immediately denounced the novelty to the Congregation and was asked to make a memorandum. It was most violent; Pius IX, to whom the memorandum was submitted in printed form, had it withdrawn. In its place the S.R.C. sent a circular letter inviting the bishops to give their reasons for the change of chasubles. As the Holy See was again consulted in 1925, the circular letter was officially published for the first time in that year.

It is not the purpose of the present work to challenge the historical authenticity of this account of the origin of the letter of 1863. Suffice it to note that the original Memorandum of Msgr. Corazza was prepared as a *Votum* on the letter of the Bishop of Munster under the date of June 10, 1859.[107]

Regarding the "official" publication of the letter of 1863, it should be noted that, although it did not appear in the *Decr. Auth.*

[107] Sacra Rituum Congregatione, Eminentissimo et Reverendissimo Cardinali Barnabó Ponente, Monasterien, revocationis seu restitutionis planetae medii aevi alias gothicae, Instante Illustrissimo et Reverendissimo Domino Episcopo Monasterien., *Votum* Joannis Corazza, Apost. Caeremoniarum Magistri, cum *Summario* (Romae, 1863). The letter of the Bishop of Munster is given in the *Summarium*, pp. 1-16.

of the S.R.C., Wernz cited the letter as his basis for the statement that new forms of vestments were not to be introduced without a previous consulting of the Holy See.[108] Furthermore, Gasparri cited the letter verbatim.[109] Both Wernz and Gasparri gave as their reference for the letter the *Collectanea S. Congregationis de Propaganda Fide,* n. 862.[110] This collection is an official one,[111] and hence, if the Letter was contained therein, it can be said to have been published officially.

As was previously noted, Gasparri held that the vestments used in various countries in his time, although different in details, were essentially the same in form. He quoted the Letter and concluded:

> *Exinde sequitur hujusmodi immutationes in forma paramentorum in genere esse illicitas, sed posse cohonestari ex gravibus rationibus, quarum judicium pertinet ad Apostolicam Sedem.*[112]

Hence, it seems well-grounded to conclude that the position of the pre-Code canonists, at least of those who made reference to the matter, was that any change from the accepted form (which form did not include Gothic, semi-Gothic, ample, full, or oval vestments)[113] was illicit without a previous consultation with the Holy See.

From the viewpoint of the law, then, either Code or pre-Code, it appears that these vestments cannot be introduced or used without the previous approval of the Holy See.

The fifth point of Nabuco's argument for the use of larger or

108 *Ius Decretalium* III, p. 145, fn. 44.

109 *De SS. Eucharistia,* n. 700.

110 The edition of the *Collectanea S. Congregationis de Propaganda Fide* (2 vols., Romae, 1907) available to the writer does not contain the Letter of 1863. However, there was an earlier edition of this work, dated 1893. Possibly this was the edition used by Gasparri and Wernz. The Letter was contained in: *Collectanea constitutionum, decretorum, indultorum ac instructionum Sanctae Sedis ad usum operariorum apostolicorum Societatis Missionum ad exteros cura moderatorum seminarii* (Parisiis, 1880), n. 442. This last work, of course, is not an official collection, but it indicates that the letter was certainly generally known as early as early as 1880.

111 Cf. Van Hove, *Prolegomena* Vol. I, Tom. I, p. 401.

112 *De SS. Eucharistia,* n. 700.

113 Cf. Corazza, *op. cit.,* p. 5.

ample vestments is the strongest that he presents. The trend of this particular point is to show that gothic vestments are a *forma recepta* in the Church today. It should be observed, however, that under point c) in this argument, Nabuco states that he considers such vestments to be officially adopted if they are used in the Cathedral of a diocese; this could scarcely be called an "official adoption" if the Holy See had not been consulted.[114] Nabuco, and those who seem to want ample vestments, make much of the point that the Holy Father himself has worn such vestments; the first time this was done was only five years after the issuance of the decree, namely on March 19, 1930. Because of this fact the proponents for ample vestments conclude: "The controversy as to its legality may be regarded as practically settled."[115] Nabuco himself admits that the Pope cannot be said to be bound to observe the liturgical laws; although it is true that Popes usually obey the laws which they themselves have made, it does not seem to be entirely logical to conclude that because the Holy Father wore gothic vestments he intended to say a "Roman Mass, in a Roman church, with *Roman* vestments.[116] Furthermore, it seems hardly correct to conclude that the occasional lawful use of one type of vestment constituted ecclesiastical tradition in the matter.

The sixth and last point of Nabuco's argument, namely, that such vestments are now being used in a great number of places, and that the Holy See has remained silent, thereby apparently at least tolerating their use, is unsound canonical reasoning. At the present time, it is true, the Holy See has remained silent for twenty-five years. If the silence persists for fifteen more years, then one may legitimately conclude that such vestments will be permitted in virtue of customary usage that has gained the legal consent of the competent ecclesiastical authority.[117]

One further point which argues against the use of gothic vestments without the permission of the Holy See is contained in the only known response of the S.R.C. relating to the matter. This is

[114] "The Form of Vestments," *ER*, CVI (1942), 252.

[115] M. A. Chapman, "The Liturgical Directions of St. Charles Borromeo," *Liturgical Arts*, VI (1937), 93.

[116] Nabuco, "The Form of Vestments," *ER*, CVI (1942), 253.

[117] Canon 27, §1.

a private Reply of the S.R.C. to the Bishop of Barcelona, which refused permission for the use of gothic vestments. It is dated June 15, 1929.[118] In this case the reply was that the vestments were to be reduced. While it is true that one cannot argue from a private response, and that in this particular case there were extraordinary circumstances, still the case intimates that Decree 4398 was considered by the S.R.C. to be in effect, and that the S.R.C. expects to be consulted on the matter.

Accordingly it appears that in virtue of Decree 4398 no new form of vestment, either larger (which is mentioned in the Letter attached to the Decree) or smaller, is to be introduced or used without a previous consulting of the Holy See.

The traditional form of the vestments which is usually referred to as Roman is rectangular in shape, with cutaway sides. The following are the suggested measurements for a Roman chasuble of ample size:

Length: 42 inches (minimum).

Width at back (across shoulders): 30 or 31 inches.

Width in front (across chest): 21 inches.

Width in front (at bottom): 27 inches.

Breadth of pillar and cross: 8 to 12 inches (including the braid which is generally about an inch wide).[119]

A chasuble made according to these dimensions and of suitable material and ornamentation can be ample, graceful, dignified, as the laws of the sacred art demand, and still be in accordance with the received usage of the Church in Rome.[120]

118 *Periodica,* XVIII (1929-30), 246.

119 Anson, *Churches,* p. 191.

120 J. O'Connell, *The Celebration of Mass,* I, 268.

A LIST OF THE SACRED FURNISHINGS NECESSARY FOR CATHEDRAL AND PARISH CHURCHES

I. Furnishings of the Altar and Sanctuary:
- Fixed altar or an altar stone for a portable altar
- Altar Cross
- Candlesticks
  - 6 for solemn Masses (7 in cathedrals)
  - 2 for low Masses
  - 2 for each side altar
  - *Bugia* (C) (Note: C in parentheses indicates that the furnishing is needed only in cathedrals)
  - 12 for solemn Exposition
  - 20 for Forty Hours
  - 6 for funerals
- Candles (same number as candlesticks)
- Cerecloth
- Lower altar cloths
- Upper altar cloth
- Frontal (1 of each color)
- Missal cushion or stand
- Vesperal
- Tabernacle veil (one of each color except black)
- Credence table and cover
- Ewer and basin (C)
- Cruets and stoppers
- Finger towel
- Communion cloth
- Communion paten
- Sanctuary lamp
- *Sanctus* bell
- *Sedilia*
- Permanent bishop's throne (C)
- Portable bishop's throne
- Chairs for bishop's assistants
- Faldstool
- Predieu
- Stools or benches for acolytes

II. Vestments

A. Proper to bishops (C)
- Tunicle
- Dalmatic
- Sandals
- Buskins
- Gloves
- Mitres: Precious, Gold, Simple
- Ring
- Crozier
- Pectoral Cross
- Gremial
- Rochet
- Morse

B. Proper to Others
- Amice
- Alb
- Cincture
- Maniple
- Stole
- Chasuble
- Cope
- Tunic
- Dalmatic
- Humeral Veil
- Guimpe (C)
- Surplice
- Broad stole
- Folded Chasuble

III. Sacred vessels and their appurtenances
- Chalice
- Paten
- Ciborium
- Monstrance
- Lunette
- *Custodia*
- Ciborium veil
- Chalice veil
- Burse
- Corporal
- Pall
- Purificator

IV. Baptismal accessories
- Holy oils
- Salt
- Ladle
- Cotton
- Stoles
- White linen garment

- Candle
- Ritual
- Towels

V. Other Furnishings

- Metropolitan Cross (only in metropolitan cathedral)
- Processional Cross
- Aspersory
- Aspergil
- Incense
- Thurible
- Boat
- Spoon for incense
- Tripod for thurible
- Oil Stocks
- Paxbrede
- Vessel for washing sacred vessels and sacred linens
- Canopy (for processions)
- *Umbella*
- Acolytes' candlesticks and torches
- Paschal candle and candlestick
- Triple candle and candlestick
- *Tenebrae* candlestick

Funeral pall

- Catalfalque

Books:

- *Missale Romanum*
- *Missale Defunctorum*
- *Rituale Romanum*
- *Pontificale Romanum*
- *Canon Pontificalis* (C)
- *Caeremoniale Episcoporum*
- *Vesperale*

CONCLUSIONS

A. Regarding the Sacred Furnishings in General

1. Before the official publication of the Liturgical Books and the establishment of the Congregation of Rites, the law on the sacred furnishings was based largely on the Decree of Gratian. This compilation contained no universal authentic legislation; its authentic canons were derived from particular councils.

2. In order to guarantee the neatness, cleanliness, and safekeeping of the sacred furnishings as demanded by the law of the Code, local ordinaries are empowered to legislate on the following matters: a) That the inventory of the sacred furnishings be resubmitted to the chancery office at least once a year; b) that a safe be provided for the sacred vessels and precious sacred furnishings; c) that the sacred vessels be thoroughly cleaned at least once a year, and that the linens and linen vestments be changed at specified intervals.

3. Sacred furnishings which have lost their consecration or blessing according to the provisions of canon 1305, §1, may be treated as non-sacred articles, and such chalices and patens may be handled by the laity, always of course to the preclusion of possible scandal or contempt.

4. Although pastors and rectors of churches are given the faculty by the law of the Code to bless sacred furnishings, they cannot delegate this faculty.

5. Regarding the provision of the sacred furnishings for use it appears to be more seemly that the bishop be permitted to use the sacred furnishings of the cathedral church wheresoever in the diocese he pontificates; priests, too, whether attached to a church or externs, should be permitted the gratuitous use of the sacred furnishings.

6. Even non-beneficed clerics should make proper provision for the transmission of their sacred furnishings upon their demise.

B. Regarding the Sacred Furnishings in Particular

The prescriptions regarding the sacred furnishings in particular are as a rule clearly contained in the Liturgical Books and in the Decrees of the Congregation of Rites. However, the following points may here be indicated as matters that are overlooked in practice:

1. The altar cross should be of the same design and material as the altar candlesticks; it should not be suspended above the altar, but should stand on the altar.

2. If the structure of the tabernacle prevents the use of a tabernacle veil, then the use of curtains before the door of the tabernacle appears better than any other divergent practice to be in accord with the law.

3. Because of long-standing custom to the contrary, the use of the antependium or frontal is no longer required in many places.

4. So-called "Gothic" or ample vestments, even in the modern form, may not be used legitimately according to the present law unless permission has been obtained from the Congregation of Rites.

BIBLIOGRAPHY

SOURCES

Acta Apostolicae Sedis, Commentarium Officiale, Romae, 1909—

Acta Ecclesiae Mediolanensis, cura et studio A. Ratti, 3 vols. in 2, Mediolani, 1890-1892.

Acta et Decreta Concilii Provincialis Portlandensis in Oregon IV, anno 1932, Portland, Ore., 1934.

Acta et Decreta Synodi Diocesanae Toletanae in America Primae, anno 1943, Toledo, Ohio, 1943.

Acta Sanctae Sedis, 41 vols. Romae, 1865-1908.

Bullarum Diplomatum et Privilegiorum Sanctorum Romanorum Pontificum Taurinensis Editio, 24 vols. et Appendix, Augustae Taurinorum, 1857-1872.

Caeremoniale Episcoporum, Clementis VIII, Innocenti X, et Benedicti XIII iussu editum, Benedicti XIV et Leonis XIII auctoritate recognitum, ed. 3a post typicam, Taurini—Romae, Marietti, 1948.

Codex Iuris Canonici Pii X Pontificis Maximi iussu digestus Benedicti Papae XV auctoritate promulgatus, Romae: Typis Polyglottis Vaticanis, 1917.

Codicis Iuris Canonici Fontes, cura Emi Petri Card. Gasparri editi, 9 vols., Romae (postea Civitate Vaticana): Typis Polyglottis Vaticanis, 1923-1939. (Vols. VII-IX ed cura et studio Emi Iustiniani Card. Serédi.)

Collectanea constitutionum, decretorum, indultorum, ac instructionum Sanctae Sedis ad usum operariorum apostolicorum Societatis Missionum ad exteros cura moderatorum seminarii, Paris, 1880.

Collectanea Sacrae Congregationis de Propaganda Fide, 2 vols., Romae, 1907.

Collectio Decretorum ad Sacram Liturgiam Spectantium ab Anno 1927 ad Annum 1946, ed. 2a., Roma: Edizioni Liturgiche, 1947.

Corpus Iuris Canonici, ed. Lipsiensis secunda, post Aemilii Richteri curas . . . instruxit Aemilius Friedberg, 2 vols., Lipsiae, 1879-1881.

Decreta Authentica Congregationis Sacrorum Rituum, ex actis eiusdem collecta eiusque auctoritate promulgata sub auspiciis Ss. Domini Nostri Leonis Papae XIII, 7 vols., Vol. I-V, Romae, 1898-1901; Vol. VI, Appendix, sub auspiciis Pii Papae X, Romae, 1912; Vol. VII, Appendix, sub auspiciis Pii Papae XI, Romae, 1927.

Decreta Authentica Congregationis Sacrorum Rituum, ex actis eiusdem collecta, cura et studio Aloysii Gardellini, ed. 3a, 4 vols., Romae, 1846.

Decretales D. Gregorii Papae IX, una cum Glossis Restitutae, Romae, 1582.

Decretum Gratiani emendatum et notationibus illustratum, una cum glossis, Romae, 1582.

FRANCIS, JOSEPH, *The Laws of Holy Mass,* New York: Sheed and Ward, 1949.

JAFFÉ, PHILLIPUS, *Regesta Pontificum Romanorum ad condita Ecclesia ad annum post Christum natum MXCXVIII,* 2am ed., correctam et auctam auspiciis Gulielmi Wattenbach curaverunt F. Kaltenbrunner (ad annum 590), P. Ewald (590-882), S. Loewenfeld (882-1198), 2 vols. in 1, Lipsiae, 1885-1888.

MANSI, IOANNES, *Sacrorum Conciliorum Nova et Amplissima Collectio,* 53 vols. in 60, Parisiis, 1901-1927.

Missale Romanum, editio III iuxta Typicam Vaticanam, New York: Benziger Brothers, 1944.

Monumenta Germaniae Historica, Legum Sectio III, Tomus I, *Concilia Aevi Merovingici* (recensuit Fredericus Maassen, Hanoverae, 1893).

PIUS XII, *Mediator Dei* (Encyclical Letter on the Sacred Liturgy), Vatican Library Translation, Washington, D. C.: National Catholic Welfare Conference, 1948.

Pontificale Romanum, Summorum Pontificum iussu editum, a Benedicto XIV et Leone XIII Pont. Max. recognitum et castigatum, Ratisbonae, 1908.

POTTHAST, A., *Regesta Pontificum Romanorum inde ab anno post Christum natum MCXCVIII ad annum MCCCIV,* 2 vols., Berolini, 1874-1875.

Rituale Romanum, Pauli V Pontificis Maximi iussu editum, aliorumque Pontificum cura recognitum atque auctoritate Pii Papae XI ad normam Codicis Iuris Canonici accomodatum, ed. iuxta typicam Vaticanam, Novi Eboraci: Benziger Brothers, 1944.

SCHROEDER, H. J., *Canons and Decrees of the Council of Trent,* St. Louis: Herder Book Co., 1941.

Sylloge praecipuorum documentorum recentium Summorum Pontificum et S. Congregationis de Propaganda Fide necnon aliarum SS. Congregationum Romanarum ad usum missionariorum, Civitate Vaticana; Typis Polyglottis Vaticanis, 1939.

Synodus Dioecesano Fargensis Prima, Milwaukee: Bruce, 1941.

AUTHORS

ADONE, ALOYSIUS, *Synopsis Canonico-Liturgica,* Neapoli, 1886.

ANDRIEU, M., *Les Ordines Romani du Haut Moyen Âge,* Louvain: Bureaux, 1931.

ANSON, PETER F., *Churches, Their Plan and Furnishing* (Revised and edited by Thomas F. Croft-Fraser and H. A. Reinhold), Milwaukee: Bruce, 1948.

AYRINHAC, H., *Administrative Legislation in the New Code of Canon Law,* London, New York, Toronto: Longmans, Green and Co., 1930.

AUGUSTINE, CHARLES, *A Commentary on the New Code of Canon Law,* 2 ed., 8 vols., St. Louis, Mo.: B. Herder Book Co., 1918-1924. Vol. VI, 1921.

BARBOSA, A., *Iuris Ecclesiastici Universi Libri Tres,* Lugduni, 1660.

BESTÉ, U., *Introductio in Codicem,* ed. alt., Collegeville, Minn.: St. John's Abbey Press, 1944.

BLAT, A., *Commentarium Textus Codicis Iuris Canonici,* 5 vols. in 6, Romae, 1919-1927. Vol. III Pars altera, 1923.

BOUIX, D., *Tractatus De Jure Liturgico,* ed. 3a, Parisiis, 1873.

BOUSCAREN, T. LINCOLN, *The Canon Law Digest,* 2 vols. and *Supplement through 1948,* Milwaukee: Bruce, 1934, 1943, 1949.

CALLEWAERT, C., *Liturgicae Institutiones, Tractatus Primus de S. Liturgia Universim,* ed. alt., Brugis: Beyaert, 1925.

CAPPELLO, F. M., *Tractatus Canonico-Moralis de Sacramentis,* 5 vols., Vol. I, ed. 4a, Romae: Marietti, 1945.

CAVANAUGH, WILLIAM T., *The Reservation of the Blessed Sacrament,* The Catholic University of America Canon Law Studies, n. 40, Washington, D. C., The Catholic University of America, 1927.

COCCHI, GUIDUS, *Commentarium in Codicem Iuris Canonici,* 8 vols. in 5, Vol. V, ed. 4a, Taurinorum Augustae: Marietti, 1942.

COLLINS, HAROLD E., *The Church Edifice and Its Appointments,* Westminster, Md.: The Newman Bookshop, 1946.

CORAZZA, IOANNES, Sacra Rituum Congregatione, Eminentissimo et Reverendissimo Cardinali Barnabó Ponente, Monasterien. revocationis seu restitutionis planetae medii aevi alias gothicae, Instante Illustrissimo et Reverendissimo Domino Episcopo Monasterien., *Votum* Joannis Corazza, Apost. Caeremoniarum Magistri, cum *Summario,* Romae, 1863.

Coronata, Matthaeus Conte A., *Institutiones Iuris Canonici*, ed. alt., 5 vols., Taurini—Romae: Marietti, 1939-1947. Vol. II, 1939.

———, *Tractatus Canonicus de Sacramentis*, 3 vols., Romae: Marietti, 1943-1946. Vol. III, 1946.

Dix, Gregory, *The Shape of the Liturgy*, Westminster, Dacre Press, 1946.

Durandus, G., *Rationale Divinorum Officiorum*, Neapoli, 1859.

Duchesne, L., *Christian Worship, Its Origin and Evolution*, New York, 1903.

Fagnanus, Prosper, *Commentaria in Quinque Libros Decretalium*, 5 vols. in 3, Venetiis, 1709-1720.

Fortescue, Adrian, *The Ceremonies of the Roman Rite Described*, 7 ed., revised by J. O'Connell, London: Burns, Oates and Washbourne, 1947.

Gasparri, Petrus, *Tractatus Canonicus de Sanctissima Eucharistia*, 2 vols., Parisiis, 1897.

Gavantus, B., *Thesaurus Sacrorum Rituum*, Venetiis, 1672.

Gennari, Cardinalis Casimirus, *Consultazioni morali, canoniche, liturgiche*, Napoli, 1893.

Hannan, Jerome D., *The Canon Law of Wills*, The Catholic University of America Canon Law Studies, n. 86, Washington, D. C.: The Catholic University of America, 1934.

Hinschius, P., *Decretales Pseudo-Isidoriannae*, Lipsiae, 1883.

Hittorpius, Melchior, *De Catholicae Ecclesiae Divinis Officiis ac Ministeriis Varii Vetustorum fere Omnium Ecclesiae Patrum ac Scriptorum Libri*, Romae, 1591.

Hostiensis, Cardinalis (Henricus de Segusio), *Commentaria in Quinque Decretalium Libros*, 5 vols. in 3, Venetiis, 1581.

———, *Summa Aurea*, Basileae, 1573.

Migne, J. P., *Patrologiae Cursus Completus, Series Latina*, 221 vols., Parisiis, 1844-1864.

Nabuco, Joaquim, *Pontificalis Romani Expositio*, 3 vols., Petropoli-Brazil: Sumptibus Editora Vozes Ltda., 1945.

Nicene and Post-Nicene Fathers of the Christian Church, 2nd Series, Vol. X, New York, 1896.

O'Connell, J., *The Celebration of Mass*, 3 vols., Milwaukee: Bruce, 1940-1941.

O'CONNELL, LAURENCE, *The Book of Ceremonies,* Milwaukee: Bruce, 1943.

PANORMITANUS, ABBAS (Nicholas de Tudeschis), *Commentaria in Quinque Libros Decretalium,* 5 vols. in 7, Venetiis, 1588.

RAYMUNDUS DE PEÑAFORTE, *Summa,* Veronae, 1744.

RAGATILLO, EDUARDUS F., *Ius Sacramentalium,* 2 vols. Sal Tarrae: Santander, 1945-46.

ROULIN, DOM E., *Modern Church Architecture,* St. Louis-London: B. Herder, 1947.

———, *Vestments and Vesture,* Westminster, Md.: The Newman Press, 1950.

SIPOS, STEPHANUS, *Enchiridion Iuris Canonici,* ed. 3a, Pecs: Ex Typographia "Haladas R. T.," 1936.

STEIDLE, BASIL, *Patrologia,* Friburgi: Heder and Co., 1937.

THOMASSINUS, LUDOVICUS, *Vetus et Nova Ecclesiae Disciplina circa Beneficia et Beneficarios,* 10 vols., Magontiaci, 1787.

THOMAS DE AQUINO, ST., *Summa Theologiae,* 5 vols., Ottawa: Studium Generale O. Pr., 1941-1945.

VAN DER STAPPEN, J. F., *Sacra Liturgia,* 3 ed., 5 vols., Mechliniae, 1911-1945.

VAN HOVE, A., *Commentarium Lovaniense in Codicem Iuris Canonici,* Vol. I, tom. 1, *Prolegomina ad Codicem Iuris Canonici,* 2 ed., Mechliniae-Romae: H. Dessain, 1945.

VERMEERSCH, A.-CREUSEN, J., *Epitome Iuris Canonici,* 6 ed., 3 vols. Mechliniae-Romae: H. Dessain, 1937-1946. Vol. II, 1940.

VROMANT, G., *De Bonis Ecclesiae Temporalibus,* Paris, 1927.

WAPELHORST, P. INNOCENTIUS, *Compendium Sacrae Liturgiae Iuxta Ritum* Romanum, 12. ed., New York: Benziger, 1945.

WERNZ, F. X., *Ius Decretalium,* 6 vol., Vol. III, 2. ed. Romae et Prati, 1908.

WERNZ, F. X.-VIDAL, P., *Ius Canonicum ad Codicis Normam Exactum,* 7 vols., in 8, Romae: apud Aedes Universitatis Gregorianae, 1923-1938. Tom. IV, Vol. 1, 1934.

WEBB, GEOFFREY, *The Liturgical Altar,* New York: Benziger, 1939.

WOYWOD, S., *A Practical Commentary on the Code of Canon Law,* 2 vols., tenth printing as edited by C. Smith, New York: J. Wagner, Inc., 1946.

ARTICLES

CHAPMAN, M. A., "The Liturgical Directions of St. Charles Borromeo," *Liturgical* Arts, VI (1937), 91-94.

CICOGNANI, H. I., "De facultate benedicendi sacram suppellectilem ex can. 1304, *Apollinaris,* I (1928), 65-66.

DEVINY, W., "Church Finance and Accounting," *ER,* Part I, LXXI (1924), 152-164; Part II, 263-271.

LARDONE, G., "Obbligo della cattedrale circa le suppellettili," *Perfice Munus,* III (1928), 48.

NABUCO, JOAQUIM, "The Form of Vestments," *ER,* CVI (1942), 241-254.

PAUWELS, J., "De forma paramentorum," *Periodica,* XV (1926-27), 58-65.

———, "La forme des ornaments liturgiques," *Revue des Communautés Religieuses,* II (1926), 71-77.

———, "La Forme des Chasubles," *Nouvelle Revue Théologique,* LIII (1926), 300-304.

TALBOT, W. R.—LALLOU, W. J., "The Textile Appurtenances of the Altar," *Liturgical Arts,* I (1931-32), 55-62.

PERIODICALS

American Ecclesiastical Review, The, vols., I-XXXII, Philadelphia, 1889-1905; from 1905: *The Ecclesiastical Review,* Vols. XXXIII-CIX, Philadelphia, 1905-1943; from 1944: *The American Ecclesiastical Review,* Washington, D. C., Vol. CX, 1944—

Apollinaris, Romae, 1928—

Liturgical Arts, New York, N. Y., 1931—

Nouvelle Revue Théologique, Paris, 1869—

Perfice Munus, Romae, 1926—

Periodica de Religiosis et Missionariis, Brugis, 1905-1919; *Periodica de Re Canonica et Morali utili praesertim Religiosis et Missionariis,* 1920-1927; *Periodica de Re Canonica, Morali, Liturgica,* 1927—

Revue des Communautés Religieuses, Louvain, 1925—

ABBREVIATIONS

AAS—Acta Apostolicae Sedis.

Acta Eccl. Mediol.—Acta Ecclesiae Mediolanensis.

AER—The American Ecclesiastical Review.

ASS—Acta Sanctae Sedis.

BRT—Bullarium Romanum, ed. Tauriensis.

Coll. Decr.—Collectio Decretorum ad Sacram Liturgiam Spectantium ab Anno 1927 ad Annum 1946.

Decr. Auth.—Decreta Authentica Congregationis Sacrorum Rituum.

ER—The Ecclesiastical Review.

Fontes—Codicis Iuris Canonici Fontes cura. Gasparri editi.

Hinschius—*Decretales Pseudo-Isidorianae.*

Jaffé E—Jaffé, *Regesta Pontificum Romanorum* (Edited by Ewald; for the years 590-582).

Jaffé K—Jaffé, *op. cit.* (Edited by Kaltenbrunner; to the year 590).

Jaffé L—Jaffé, *op. cit.* (Edited by Loewenfeld; for the years 882-1198).

Mansi—*Sacrorum Conciliorum Nova et Amplissima Collectio.*

MPL.—Migne, *Patrologia Latina.*

Periodica—Periodica de Re morali, Canonica, Liturgica.

Potthast—*Regesta Pontificum Romanorum,* etc.

S.R.C.—Sacrorum Rituum Congregatio.

Sylloge—Sylloge praecipuorum documentorum recentium Summorum Pontificum et S. Congregationis de Propaganda Fide necnon aliarum SS. Congregationum Romanarum, etc.

BIOGRAPHICAL NOTE

Erwin L. Sadlowski was born on January 10, 1913, at Grand Rapids, Michigan. He attended St. Adalbert and St. Anthony Parochial Schools in that city. In 1926 he entered St. Joseph Seminary, Grand Rapids, Michigan, and was graduated in 1932. In September of that year he was admitted to Basselin Foundation, The Catholic University of America, Washington, D. C., where he received his A.B. degree in 1934, and M.A. in philosophy in 1935. He pursued his course of Theological Studies at the Sulpician Seminary, Catholic University of America. He was ordained to the Holy Priesthood on April 16, 1939, for the Diocese of Spokane, Washington. In that diocese, he served as an assistant and pastor until May, 1943, when he entered the United States Navy as a chaplain for the duration of the war. After the completion of his tour of duty in the Navy in 1946, he entered the School of Canon Law at the Catholic University of America, Washington, D. C. He received the degree of the Baccalaureate in Canon Law in June, 1947, and the Licentiate in Canon Law the following year.

Altar properly furnished when there is no tabernacle. cf. pp. 84 sqq.

Altar properly furnished when there is a tabernacle. cf. pp. 84 sqq.

ALPHABETICAL INDEX

www.ingramcontent.com/pod-product-compliance
Lightning Source LLC
LaVergne TN
LVHW050234080826
844660LV00012B/531

* 9 7 8 0 8 1 3 2 2 4 9 0 9 *